Cambridge Elements

Elements in the Philosophy of Immanuel Kant
edited by
Desmond Hogan
Princeton University
Howard Williams
University of Cardiff
Allen Wood
Indiana University

KANT ON THE RATIONALITY OF MORALITY

Paul Guyer
Brown University

CAMBRIDGE
UNIVERSITY PRESS

University Printing House, Cambridge CB2 8BS, United Kingdom

One Liberty Plaza, 20th Floor, New York, NY 10006, USA

477 Williamstown Road, Port Melbourne, VIC 3207, Australia

314–321, 3rd Floor, Plot 3, Splendor Forum, Jasola District Centre,
New Delhi – 110025, India

79 Anson Road, #06–04/06, Singapore 079906

Cambridge University Press is part of the University of Cambridge.

It furthers the University's mission by disseminating knowledge in the pursuit of education, learning, and research at the highest international levels of excellence.

www.cambridge.org
Information on this title: www.cambridge.org/9781108438810
DOI: 10.1017/9781108529761

First published 2019

A catalogue record for this publication is available from the British Library.

ISBN 978-1-108-43881-0 Paperback
ISSN 2514-3824 (print)
ISSN 2397-9461 (online)

Kant on the Rationality of Morality

Elements in the Philosophy of Immanuel Kant

DOI: 10.1017/9781108529761
First published online: July 2019

Paul Guyer
Brown University, Rhode Island

Author for correspondence: Paul Guyer paul_guyer@brown.edu

Abstract: Kant claims that the fundamental principle of morality is given by pure reason itself. Many have interpreted Kant to derive this principle from a conception of pure practical reason (as opposed to merely prudential reasoning about the most effective means to empirically given ends). But Kant maintained that there is only one faculty of reason, although with both theoretical and practical applications. This Element shows how Kant attempted to derive the fundamental principle and goal of morality from the general principles of reason as such. To achieve this, it takes reason as Kant himself conceived of it, namely, as defined above all by the two fundamental principles of noncontradiction and sufficient reason, with a third principle of systematicity attached to the second of these. Its main argument is that Kant attempted to derive the fundamental principle of morality in its several formulations by applying the principle of noncontradiction to the fact that human beings are agents with their own wills, and the complete object of morality, the highest good, from the principle of sufficient reason. Further, Kant supposed both that the application of the fundamental principle of morality must be systematic, thus yielding a system of duties, and also that morality itself must be part of a complete system of both theoretical and practical cognition, or more precisely part of the ideal of such a complete system of cognition. Kant also held that pure reason is practical, in the sense of being able to motivate human beings to action; the Element will also consider his theoretical justification of this claim and its empirical consequences.

Keywords: Kant, duty, freedom, fundamental principle of morality, highest good, humanity, principle of noncontradiction, practical reason, principle of sufficient reason, systematicity, the unconditioned

ISBNs: 9781108438810 (PB), 9781108529761 (OC)
ISSNs: 2397-9461 (online), 2514-3824 (print)

Contents

1 Introduction

Immanuel Kant claims that the fundamental principle of morality is given by pure reason itself. His *Groundwork of the Metaphysics of the Morals*, published in 1785, starts with the statement that "a law, if it is to hold morally, that is, as a ground of an obligation ... must not be sought in the nature of the human being or in the circumstances of the world in which he is placed, but *a priori* simply in concepts of pure reason" (G 4: 389). He later grounds its central argument that the moral law does apply to us human beings on the claim that we do have reason: "a human being really finds in himself a capacity by which he distinguishes himself from all other things, even from himself insofar as he is affected by objects, and that is *reason*" (G 4: 452). The *Critique of Practical Reason*, published in 1788 in order to defend the *Groundwork*, states that its "first question" will be whether "pure reason of itself alone suffices to determine the will or whether it can be a determining ground of the will only as empirically conditioned," and decisively opts for the first of these alternatives: "reason can at least suffice to determine the will and always has objective reality insofar as volition alone is at issue" (CPrR 5: 15). By this Kant means, first, that pure reason by itself suffices to furnish the fundamental principle of morality by which the human will *ought* to be determined – in Kant's model of human action, in the agent's selection of particular maxims, suggested by experience, upon which to act in particular circumstances – and, second, that pure reason, by itself, can suffice to *motivate* human beings to act as they ought to act.[1]

[1] Kant's division of the cognitive powers or "faculties" of human beings evolved over his career, and his use of his own terminology was often flexible. His most fundamental distinction was between sensibility and intellect, with the former being our receptivity to representations from external objects or internal states and the latter our ability to organize our thought about such representations. Our most immediate representations of particular objects are called intuitions (*Anschauungen*), and our general representations of objects by means of marks that particular objects may share are called concepts. From the *Critique of Pure Reason* (first edition 1781) onward, Kant generally divides intellect into understanding and reason: understanding is the ability to form concepts and apply them either to particular objects or to other concepts in judgments, although in the *Critique of the Power of Judgment* (1790) Kant elevates judgment to a separate faculty; reason is, in the first instance, the ability to concatenate judgments, for example, in inferences. Sensibility, understanding, judgment, and reason all have characteristic forms that are not derived from experience but are applied to experience through empirically given intuitions: the pure forms of space and time in the case of sensibility, the pure categories of the understanding, and the pure ideas of reason, namely first the forms of inference and then the unconditioned ideas of the soul, the world-whole, and God. We can have *a priori* knowledge of the structure of the pure forms of sensibility and understanding, and these forms are also the forms of empirical knowledge. If reason is applied to our representations of how things are in the form of intuitions, concepts, and judgments, it is theoretical reason; if it is applied to our representations of how our own actions could bring about what ought to be, it is practical reason. The attempt to know what is through the theoretical use of reason alone would be speculative reason, and in Kant's view is a failure, because the unconditioned ideas of reason by their very nature outstrip anything that can be given in experience; however, the attempt to determine how we ought to act

Sometimes Kant seems to go even further than these claims, already bold enough, to assert that the human will and pure reason are *identical*, as when he says that "the will is nothing other than practical reason" (G 4: 412). This remark has led many to ask how Kant could possibly explain voluntary but *immoral* behavior if he identifies reason as the source of *both* the moral law and all willed action: How could a will that as pure reason gives itself the moral law then act on any ground other than that?[2] But Kant clarifies this statement so quickly that no one should be misled by it, for when he makes it he is explaining why principles of reason, valid for all rational beings, present themselves *to us human beings* as *imperatives*:[3] "If reason infallibly determines the will," he continues, then "the will is a capacity to choose **only that** which reason independently of inclination cognizes as practically necessary, that is, as good," but "if the will is not **in itself** completely in conformity with reason (as is actually the case with human beings)," then the will is *not* identical with practical reason and what pure reason requires of us can appear to us as a constraint or "necessitation" (*Nötigung*) (G 4: 412). Human beings can have inclinations – empirically given desires – toward actions contrary to what morality requires, so what morality requires can come across to us as a constraint. Likewise, the passage quoted from the *Critique of Practical Reason* implies only that pure reason is *capable* of determining how the human will *should* act, hardly that it determines how the human will or human being always *does* act. To be sure, even this more limited claim was a bold one for Kant to make when David Hume had argued that moral principles must be grounded in sentiment rather than reason precisely because "morals" must "have an influence on the actions and affections" and "reason alone . . . can never have any such influence."[4] Later we will consider some aspects of Kant's theory that pure reason is capable of moving creatures like us even though we

---

by reason alone would be the pure use of practical reason, or pure practical reason, and because it does not purport to tell us how the actual world is but how it ought to be, it is in Kant's view a success. Finally, the human ability to determine action is called "will" (*Wille*), but Kant will ultimately divide that into two parts: the ability to furnish principles of action (*Wille*) and the ability to choose which principles to act upon (the power of choice or *Willkür*). Pure *Wille* is identical to pure practical reason and provides the moral law. For Kant's distinctions, see especially CPR A19-20/B33-4, A298-302/B355-9, and A320/B376-7, as well as CPrR 5: 37 and 15–16.

[2] This question was raised in Kant's own time by Johann August Heinrich Ulrich (1746–1813) in Ulrich 1788, and a hundred years later by Henry Sidgwick in Sidwick 1888. For contemporary discussion, see Wuerth 2014, ch. 7, and Guyer 2018a.

[3] The validity of the moral law for all rational beings does not commit Kant to the actual *existence* of any rational beings other than human beings; its validity for other *possible* rational beings is intended to guarantee that the moral law is not grounded on merely contingent aspects of human nature.

[4] Hume 1739–40, Book 3, Part 1, Section 1, paragraph 6.

have all sorts of desires to act otherwise than as morality demands. But our first question is simply, how did Kant think that pure reason of itself can provide the fundamental principle of morality? Or, more fully, how did he think that reason can determine the fundamental principle and the proper "object" of morality, that is, the goal of morality? How can reason alone determine even what we *ought* to try to do and accomplish in the name of morality? What *is* reason, in Kant's view, that it can do *that*?

Kant does talk about "practical reason." Obviously: The title of his second critique is the *Critique of Practical Reason*, and its aim is "to show *that there is pure practical reason*, and for this purpose it criticizes reason's entire *practical faculty*" (CPrR 5: 3). By practical reason Kant means reason insofar as it bears on volition and action, thus on our choice of principles for action and our motivation by those principles, and his argument that there *is* such a thing as pure practical reason is intended to show that the application of reason to action is not limited to providing merely technical advice[5] on what means to use to achieve ends that are set for us by desire, as Hume had asserted in his *Treatise*.[6] Kant's position is that reason can give us moral principles and set our moral goals on its own, as well as motivate us to act in accordance with these. But Kant also insists that "there can, in the end, be only one and the same reason, which may be distinguished merely in its application" (G 4: 391). That is, Kant does not suppose that practical reason is a faculty distinct from theoretical reason, or that practical reason has a special form or special forms for reasoning about action that can be understood apart from our forms for reasoning in general. For Kant, the principles that determine how we should act are fundamental to reason as such.

To be sure, there are differences between the application of reason to matters of fact and to matters of action. For one, in the theoretical use of reason we reason about how things *are*, while in the practical use of reason we reason about how things *ought* to be: "insofar as there is to be reason . . . something must be cognized *a priori*, and this cognition can relate to its object in either of two ways, either merely **determining the object** and its concept (which must be given from elsewhere), or else also **making** the object actual. The former is **theoretical**, the latter **practical** cognition of reason" (CPR Bix-x). For another, and this is the conclusion of Kant's entire philosophy, there are things the reality of which cannot be asserted on the basis of a strictly theoretical use of reason, namely the existence of God and of our own freedom and immortality.

[5] Kant calls technical advice given by (empirical) reason on how to realize goals that are set not by reason itself but by desire "hypothetical imperatives," "imperatives of skill," or "technical" imperatives (G 4: 416–17).

[6] See Hume 1739–40, Book 3, Part 1, Section 1, paragraph 12.

The theoretical use of reason is restricted by the limits of sensibility, that is, by what we can actually perceive, and we cannot perceive God or our own freedom or immortality; yet, Kant holds, we are nevertheless entitled to affirm the existence of these things on the basis of the practical use of reason. This is because he thinks that it "would be absolutely impossible" for us to act in accordance with the fundamental principle of morality if we could not "presuppose" the existence of freedom, God, and our own immortality as necessary conditions for the possibility of moral success, and these things are in any case not *disproven* by the theoretical use of reason (CPR Bxxviii); or, if "practical reason has of itself original *a priori* principles with which certain theoretical positions are inseparably connected . . . then it is clear that, even if from the first perspective [reason's] capacity does not extend to establishing certain propositions affirmatively, although they do not contradict it, **as soon as these same propositions belong inseparably to the practical interest** of pure reason it must accept them." In this sense the practical use of reason has "primacy" over its theoretical use, "assuming that this union is not **contingent** and discretionary but based *a priori* on reason itself and therefore **necessary**" (CPrR 5: 121). So there is certainly something distinctive about practical reason for Kant, namely, that once the fundamental principle of morality and its necessary goal have been determined, we are entitled to hold beliefs about the conditions for the successful realization of morally mandated action that we would not be entitled to hold on theoretical grounds alone. To that extent it makes sense to talk of practical reason as a distinctive form of reason in Kant's theory.

But Kant claims this special entitlement for practical reason to affirm the conditions of the possibility of realizing the goals that morality sets for us only *after* he has derived the fundamental principle of morality from reason as such, not from any special kind of reason but simply from the application of the principles of reason in general to the case of action. One and the same reason that gives us the most fundamental principle of principles for thinking about what is, Kant claims, also gives us the most fundamental principle for deciding how we may and must act. Our first question, then, is how does Kant think that reason as such yields the fundamental principle of morality?

2 Reasons, Reasoning, and Reason as Such

I am stressing Kant's ambition to derive the fundamental principle of morality from the principles of *reason in general* because many philosophers have recently attempted to derive morality from conceptions of *practical reason* as a distinct form of reason. I will consider several examples of the latter approach in this section before turning to my own interpretation of Kant in the following one. For example, Christine Korsgaard has stated that the fundamental thing that "arises from our rational nature" is "our need to have reasons." Here she has defined rationality on the basis of an antecedent conception of reasons.[7] But she has said several things about what a reason is or what it is to have a reason. In *The Sources of Normativity* (1996), she presented as Kantian the requirement that "Each impulse as it offers itself to the will must pass a kind of test for normativity before we can adopt it as a reason for action," and "the test is one of reflective endorsement."[8] So a reason is not a reason all by itself, like a tree falling in a forest whether anyone hears it or not; rather, an inclination – any sort of desire to act that might naturally happen to present itself to a human being[9] – toward an action becomes a reason for action only once it has been endorsed as such by an agent capable of a certain kind of reflection.[10] That just pushes the question of what a reason is back to the questions, what kind of agent and what kind of reflection? In *The Sources of Normativity*, Korsgaard argued that Kant's own test for what could be a moral principle, simply that it have "the form of a law . . . *All that it has to be is a law*," can be improved.[11] Thus she argued first that agents reflectively transform impulses into reasons from the standpoint of some "practical identity," such as that of a being "a member of a certain religion, a member of an ethnic group, a member of a certain profession, someone's lover or friend, and so on," each of which "identities gives rise to reasons and obligations": If one thinks of oneself as having such an identity, then "[y]our reasons express your identity, your nature; your obligations spring from what that identity forbids."[12] But some if not all of these identities do not and cannot give rise to universally valid reasons and obligations: all too obviously not all human beings are adherents of the same religion or ethnic group – if they were, many of the most savage moments of human history would never have occurred – neither is everyone, nor can they be, members of the same profession, and so on. So these kinds of practical identities were only a first step in Korsgaard's argument; she went on to argue that reflectively endorsing any of these kinds of *particular* practical identities

[7] Korsgaard 2009, p. 24. [8] Korsgaard 1996b, p. 91.

[9] In his 1798 *Anthropology from a Pragmatic Point of View* Kant defines an inclination (*Neigung*) as a "habitual sensible desire" (Anth, §73, 7: 251). But in his writings in moral philosophy he often speaks of inclination without any suggestion that it must be habitual (e.g., G 4: 397–8, 400), instead defining it simply as the representation or thought of pleasure or satisfaction or the opposite from the existence of some object or state of affairs (CPrR 5: 21–3). I follow Kant in using the term in this more general sense.

[10] This is what Henry Allison had previously called the "Incorporation Thesis," the thesis that the mere occurrence of an inclination does not determine the will, but rather only its "incorporation" into a maxim of a rational agent does, that is, its "being taken by the agent (at least implicitly) as [a] sufficient reason . . . for action"; Allison 1990, p. 126.

[11] Korsgaard 1996b, p. 98. [12] Korsgaard 1996b, p. 101.

depends upon recognizing that no matter what particular practical identity you endorse you must also endorse "your identity simply as a *human being*, a reflective animal who needs reasons to act and to live." Korsgaard further argued, "And so it is a reason you have only if you treat your humanity as a practical, normative, form of identity, that is, if you value yourself as a human being," and then she took human identity as such in *anyone* as something that gives reasons for *everyone* to treat that general identity *in anyone* as a fundamental source of normativity, as giving everyone reason to act in certain ways and not in others. "If this is right," she concluded, "our identity as moral beings – as people who value themselves as human beings – stands behind our more particular practical identities. It is because we are human that we must act in the light of practical conceptions of our identity, and this means that their importance is partly derived from the importance of being human."[13]

This argument explicitly makes one strong assumption about rationality, namely that what it is to be human is (at least in part) to require sound reasons for one's actions; and it makes another strong assumption implicitly, namely that a genuine reason for *anyone* is a genuine reason for *everyone* – that my identity as a requirer of reasons in general, in which the normative force of any particular practical identity that I may recognize is grounded, is also a reason for anyone to recognize my right to act on my own reasons, whether they share or endorse my particular practical identity or not. Korsgaard is more explicit about this second requirement in a more recent book, *Self-Constitution* (2009). Here she argues that a creature who acted without reasons would not be a unified agent, a person, at all, only a "heap" of impulses, or, more realistically, that "it seems rather *obvious* that a formal principle for balancing our various ends and reasons must be a principle for unifying our agency ... so that we are not always tripping over ourselves when we pursue our various projects, so that our agency is not incoherent."[14] To prevent incoherence among our projects, or the impulses that suggest them, reasons cannot be "completely particular," as they would be if it were "possible to have a reason that applies only to the case before you, and has no implications for any other case."[15] But what Korsgaard infers from this is that a genuine reason cannot be merely *general* – that is, perhaps

---

13 Korsgaard 1996b, p. 121.

14 Korsgaard 2009, p. 58. In fact, it is far from *obvious* that a human being must possess a unified representation or conception of herself. Adrian Piper has argued that Kant's view that a moral *agent* must be unified derives from his complex argument that a human *subject* must possess what Kant calls "transcendental unity of apperception," a (second-order) representation (or the possibility of one; see CPR B132) that all her (first-order) representations constitute representations of a single, unified self, and that this requires the use of concepts; see Piper 2013, volume II. For my own interpretation of Kant's concept of apperception and the transcendental deduction, see Guyer 1987, Part II.

15 Korsgaard 2009, pp. 72–3.

valid only for one or some agents, and perhaps only for some period of time – but must be genuinely *universal* – that is, valid for *any* person (at least in a certain kind of situation) *all* of the time. Reasons "are universal," although "universality is quite compatible with – indeed it requires – a high degree of specificity";[16] that is, a reason need not, indeed could not possibly be valid for everyone in any kind of situation, but it must be valid for anyone in a certain kind of situation. Thus Korsgaard concludes that reasons are "considerations that have normative force for *me* as well as you," and *vice versa*, and therefore reasons are by definition public reasons[17] – that is how she gets the moral law requiring universal validity out of the conditions of rational *self*-constitution. This argument clearly depends upon the assumption that anything that is a reason is universally valid: Korsgaard does not use the notion of a reason as an undefined primitive, but does take the requirement that a reason is a universally rather than merely generally valid ground for, or consideration in behalf of action to be self-evident, and derives the moral law as the condition of coherent agency at all by means of this assumption. So she does define reason in terms of a certain conception of rationality, namely that rationality requires universal validity.[18]

Allen Wood forthrightly identifies a reason with a universally valid norm and defines reason in terms of such reasons. Thus he defines reason as "the capacity to think and act according to *norms*" and "[a] *reason*, in the widest sense of the term," in turn, as "whatever counts as normative for beings with the capacity to give themselves norms and follow the valid norms they recognize." Thus "Reason is the faculty through which we recognize beliefs, desires, or choices as grounded on something with normative authority"; reason or rationality is therefore simply the capacity to respond to reasons.[19] But a norm is itself defined by the requirement of universal validity. For Wood defines reasons themselves – "as distinct from impulses or inclinations" – as "inherently objective or universal in their validity."[20] Thus reason is defined by its demand for universal validity, indeed as the capacity to be determined by the requirement of universal validity itself, and reasons are then defined as considerations in behalf of action that satisfy the standard of universalizability, that is, being determinative for anyone in the relevant circumstances. Or to put it more generously, on Wood's approach the concept of reasons turns out to depend upon an antecedent concept of reason after all, but reason is simply defined as our demand for universal validity. As Wood has put it more recently, "rational principles are always valid, valid equally for all rational beings. Their ultimate

[16] Korsgaard 2009, p. 73. [17] Korsgaard 2009, p. 192.

[18] For criticism of Korsgaard's move from personal to universal validity, see Wuerth 2014, pp. 291–2.

[19] Wood 2008, pp. 16–17. [20] Wood 2008, p. 16.

validity is not dependent on anything (such as contingent desires or the choice of ends) that might distinguish one rational being from another."[21]

That reason demands universal validity also turns out to be the key to Onora O'Neill's approach, although she takes the notion of *reasoning* rather than of *reasons* as her starting point. O'Neill writes:

> Two features frame all of Kant's discussions of reason. The first is his insistence that there is no independently given "canon of reason" that sets the standard for human reason. The second is his thought that since we have not been given standards for reasoning we must construct them, and that this is a shared task, to be undertaken by a plurality of free agents.[22]

Contrary to Korsgaard, and in my view *correctly*, O'Neill does not take this to be a characterization specifically of *practical* reason, but of reason in general; as she says, "reason's principles" or "precepts must apply both to thinking and doing. Kant often stresses the basic unity of theoretical and practical uses of reason."[23] But she then goes on to assert a thesis that is un-Kantian and in my view incorrect, namely that reason in general does not assume or need "antecedently established, 'eternal' standards," but rather that we "invent or construct standards for reasoned thinking and acting, standards that have the sort of generally recognized authority that we would look to find in anything that could count as a requirement of reason." It is "only when free agents discipline their thinking and acting in ways that others can follow [that] their thought and practice exemplify the fundamental, if meagre, requirements of reason."[24] This purports to be a purely procedural conception of reason or rationality: Whatever beliefs or principles of action survive the thoroughgoing attempt to accept only beliefs or principles that others can "follow" or accept count as rational, and reason is nothing other than the activity of employing this process or the capacity to do so. "Self-legislation," in turn, "is not then a mysterious phrase for describing the merely arbitrary ways in which a free individual might or might not think, but a characteristic of thinking that free individuals achieve by imposing the discipline of lawlikeness, so making their thought or their proposals for action followable by or accessible to others."[25] Consequently "the only thought or action that can count as reasoned is that which we structure by imposing the 'form of law' – of universality,"[26] and what morality requires is simply that we impose this requirement of rationality on our proposals for action or, in Kant's terms, our proposed maxims for action. O'Neill insists that "principles of reason and of logic are distinct," although "logic is abstracted either from the use of the understanding or from that of reason," so "its

[21] Wood 2014, p. 43. [22] O'Neill 2004, p. 187. [23] O'Neill 1992, p. 21.
[24] O'Neill 2004, pp. 187. [25] O'Neill 2004, p. 189. [26] O'Neill 2004, p. 189.

vindication would have to be derived from theirs, rather than conversely,"[27] as if the vindication of reason itself could proceed without any antecedent principles.

But O'Neill's characterization of reason as requiring that we make our beliefs and proposals for action followable by others belies that idea, since it treats the requirement of followability – universality – as a given – and if not given by reason itself, then by what? In other words, O'Neill treats not the concept of reasoning but that of reason (although not just practical reason) as the primitive, and explicates it in terms of the requirement for universality or universal validity. This is revealed when O'Neill makes "three substantive points" about reason: that "the discipline of reason is *negative*; second, it is *self-discipline*; third, it is a *law-giving*," which entails that the "discipline of reason . . . is at least lawlike."[28] The self-disciplining function of reason depends upon its demand for lawlikeness, because we humans are not always naturally disposed to satisfy that requirement. But this function of reason presupposes that it does require lawlikeness and can be defined as such.

O'Neill might seem to lend credibility to her claim that Kant's conception of reason does not presuppose logic or any other "eternal" standard when she remarks that "he constantly rejects conceptions of reason, such as the Principle of Sufficient Reason, which supposedly give sufficient instructions for all thinking and acting . . . His insistence that 'reason is no dictator' reiterates the thought that there is no algorithm that fully determines the content of reasoned thought and action."[29] Kant certainly does not suppose that the requirement of universal validity and the principle of sufficient reason are *sufficient* conditions for determining the full range of either human theoretical beliefs or of human duties; for the latter as well as the former we need further, empirical information about human nature and the human condition (see MM, Introduction, 6: 217). Moreover, for certain of our duties, those that he calls "imperfect" duties such as the duties to cultivate our own talents or assist others in their pursuits of happiness, Kant is clear that no rule can ever mechanically determine precisely how we should fulfill these very general obligations. But this does not mean that Kant does not treat formal principles of reason – very much including the principle of sufficient reason, as we will see – as *necessary* conditions of *reasoning* because they are the fundamental principles of *reason*. That is exactly what he does.

Korsgaard, Wood, and O'Neill thus all accept the requirement of universality as a fundamental standard of *reason* that constrains what can count as *reasons* or *reasoning* for us, in spite of having tried to define the former in terms of the

[27] O'Neill 1992, pp. 14–15. [28] O'Neill 1992, pp. 27–8. [29] O'Neill 1992, p. 28.

latter. There can be no doubt that Kant too thinks of the requirement of universal validity as intimately connected with reason as such – but since Kant thinks that the pure forms of sensibility (space and time) and the categories of the understanding (substance, causality, and so on) also give rise to universality, more precisely to necessity and universality, he cannot himself take the demand for universality to suffice to define reason because it is not unique to reason. Further, the requirement of universality must be applied to something specific in order to yield specifically moral results. This is recognized in the earliest of recent attempts to develop a moral philosophy inspired by Kant, that offered by Thomas Nagel in *The Possibility of Altruism* (1970). Nagel's thesis is that "[a]ltruism . . . depends on a recognition of the reality of other persons, and on the equivalent capacity to regard oneself as merely one individual among many."[30] His basic idea is that if one regards oneself from an "impersonal standpoint," just as one person among all others, and regards any person as having good reasons for (some) actions, then one will recognize that one has just as much reason to promote anyone's actions as one has to promote one's own. Altruism will be the immediate consequence of the application of the demand for universality to the fact of being a person. But this leaves the concept of a person underspecified. Nagel recognizes that for Kant "[i]t is the conception of ourselves as free which [is] to be the source of our acceptance of the imperatives of morality," and compares but contrasts this to his own approach dependent only on the concept of a person: "On Kant's view . . . the agent's metaphysical conception of himself" that occupies "the central role in the operation of moral motives . . . is that of freedom, but on [Nagel's] view it is the conception of oneself as merely a person among others equally real."[31] Nagel clearly thinks that his foundation is less controversial and therefore more secure than Kant's. But Kant's view, I will suggest, is that the concept of a person has to be specified before it can play a foundational role for morality, and that it is to be specified precisely as that of an agent capable of setting his or her own ends. Applying the fundamental form of reason to the fact that persons are capable of setting their own ends is what will yield the fundamental principle of morality.

But it will also be central to my interpretation of Kant not that it is wrong to recognize that reason demands universality, as all of these versions of Kantian-style moral philosophy going back to Nagel have recognized, but that for Kant himself this demand is grounded in even more fundamental principles of reason, beginning with the law of *noncontradiction* – that is, the requirement to avoid self-contradiction as a condition of successfully asserting anything at all, let alone anything that others can follow or with which they can agree. Since

[30] Nagel 1970, p. 3. [31] Nagel 1970, pp. 12, 14.

anything follows from a contradiction, a person who asserts a contradiction is asserting nothing at all: A person who says "It is raining and it is not raining" is not saying anything that another person could decide to follow. Since we cannot think at all without accepting the law of noncontradiction, we cannot think rationally without accepting this law – whatever else thinking rationally, whether about belief or action, might require.

One approach to interpreting Kant's ethics that clearly recognizes that reason does not simply start with a demand for universal validity is that of Adrian Piper. She rather equates reason with the whole intellectual structure of human cognition, and argues that all of the intellectual demands placed on cognition in general must also be placed on human actions. Thus for her (Kantian) "[r]eason consists in the familiar law-governed operations of logical analysis, generalization, deductive and inductive inference, hypothesis formation and application. These enable us to organize and unify the data of experience under higher-order concepts, principles, ideas and theories through judgment."[32] From all of this arises the requirement that the actions, or willings of action, of an agent constitute on the one hand a unified self (in Kant's terms, that they satisfy the conditions for the transcendental unity of apperception), and on the other a coherent system of willings.[33] Piper has worked out this approach with great rigor and more detail than can be matched in this Element, and I have learned a great deal from it. What I will be arguing here, however, differs from her approach in taking as Kant's starting point not just the concept of willed action but the conception of persons as capable of freely setting their own ends, indeed the fact that human beings are such persons,[34] and in restricting the fundamental principles of reason, which she construes as broadly as all of our intellectual activity, to the laws of noncontradiction and sufficient reason as well as the demand for systematicity. Further, I will argue that seeing Kant's moral philosophy as founded on those principles actually yields more of its content than Piper's approach does. While she aims to show how Kant's first formulation of the categorical imperative – the requirement that we act only on maxims that we could also will to be universal laws – follows from the structure of reason, I will show first how Kant thought that the *requirement* that we act only on universalizable maxims follows from the *fact* that human

---

[32] Piper 2012, p. 221.

[33] Piper has developed the first leg of this argument in Piper 2013, volume II, as already noted; a concise statement of the second leg can be found in Piper 1997.

[34] Although in Piper 2012, unlike some of her other writings, Piper does state that "if an event really is an action rather than mere behavior, its ultimate explanatory first principle is always the same, namely one's freedom to determine one's own actions in light of reason's demands at that time and place" (p. 225). Here her view comes closest to mine.

beings are all capable of setting their own ends. Then I will demonstrate how central elements of Kant's moral philosophy – namely his conception of the highest good as the complete object of morality, his system of duties, and his system of nature and freedom, or theoretical and moral philosophy – are all supposed to follow from the most fundamental principles of reason.

3 From Noncontradiction to Universalizability

Kant's first formulation of the "categorical imperative,"[35] that is, the constraining form in which the fundamental principle of morality presents itself to us imperfectly rational human beings, who do not always want to obey it (G 4: 412–13), is the requirement that any morally permissible maxim be universalizable, that is, consistently adoptable by all agents in circumstances similar to those in which one agent proposes to act upon it. Thus at the end of Section I of the *Groundwork*, Kant derives the categorical imperative from the exclusion of "every impulse that could arise for" the will "from obeying some law" and infers that "nothing is left but the conformity of actions as such with universal law," that is, the "principle . . . **I ought never to act except in such a way that I could also will that my maxim should become a universal law**" (G 4: 402), where a maxim is a "subjective" principle of action, the principle on which an agent actually proposes to act (G 4: 421n.). In the *Critique of Practical Reason* Kant likewise suggests that reason gives rise to the moral law by demanding no less but no more than universal validity: "it is requisite to reason's lawgiving that it should need to presuppose only **itself**, because a rule is objectively and universally valid only when it holds without the contingent, subjective conditions that distinguish one rational being from another" (CPrR 5: 21); in other words, one's maxim must be objectively as well as subjectively valid. These statements seem to support the view of many interpreters that the foundation of Kant's moral philosophy is the premise that reason demands universal validity and thus rejects any contingent ground for maxims of action. Reason's demand for universal validity in turn leads to the demand that the categorical imperative concern only the form of maxims: "If a rational being is to think of his maxims as practical universal laws, he can think of them only as principles that contain the determining ground of the will

[35] Piper has tabulated forty-seven formulations of the categorical imperative from Kant's published works in Piper 2012, pp. 260–75. I regard these as forty-seven *statements* of the categorical imperative, and reserve the term "formulation" for what Kant himself referred to as "formulas" (*Formeln*) of the categorical imperative, of which he typically suggests there are *three* (G 4: 432, 436), although he clearly formulates the third of these in two significantly different ways, one using the concept of autonomy (4: 432) and the other that of a "realm of ends" (4: 433); see also Wood 2017.

not by their matter but only by their form," for "all that remains of a law if one separates from it everything material, that is, every object of the will (as its determining ground), is the mere **form** of giving universal law" (CPrR 5: 27). Again, pure practical reason seems to begin with the demand for universal validity in our maxims of action, or that "moral laws are to hold for every rational being as such" (G 4: 412).

Yet Kant does not say that the requirement of universal validity is itself the first principle of reason. He does say that a moral law, like any law, must be universally valid, and therefore cannot be grounded in anything contingent, like any particular person's conception of happiness at any given moment (CPrR 5: 24), but must be founded in reason instead. Specifically, a genuinely *universal* claim must be founded in some genuine *necessity*, so there must be something necessary in reason that gives rise to a universally valid law. In the Preface to the *Groundwork*, Kant states that the universality of a genuine moral principle must consist in its validity for *all rational beings*, and that this must be founded in a purely rational *concept* of a rational being as such:

> Everyone must grant that a law, if it is to hold morally, that is, as a ground of an obligation, must carry with it absolute necessity; that, for example, the command "thou shalt not lie" does not hold only for human beings, as if other rational beings did not have to heed it, and so with all other moral laws properly so called; that, therefore the ground of obligation here must not be sought in the nature of the human being or in the circumstances of the world in which he is placed, but *a priori* simply in concepts of pure reason. (G 4: 389)

Kant indeed assumes that the fundamental principle of morality must be universally valid – valid for all humans in the same circumstances, not because of anything specific to human nature, but rather because of something that humans would share with any possible rational agents – but he also supposes that the requirement of universal validity itself has to be grounded in even more fundamental principles of reason. And the first of these is the principle of noncontradiction.

However, the law of noncontradiction by itself is a purely formal prohibition of contradictions, and it yields nothing concrete unless it is applied to something – it is a form that must be applied to some matter. In the first instance, the law of noncontradiction is applied to concepts to ensure that they are concepts of something that is logically *possible*; but in the second instance, the law of noncontradiction must be applied to *propositions*, or in Kant's terminology *judgments* (in particular to compound judgments), of the apparent form "*p* & *q*," in order to ensure that they are not actually contradictions, of the form "*p* & not-*p*." But the law of noncontradiction itself does not determine *which* of a pair of contradictory judgments, *p* and not-*p*, is the true one and which is the false one: that is going to require an independent ground to assert either *p* or not-*p*. The passage last quoted thus suggests only the first step of Kant's argument from the law of noncontradiction to the fundamental principle of morality. It states that the ground of obligation must be sought in *concepts of pure reason*, and those will turn out to be the (singular) pure concept of a human being as a *rational agent* – not merely rational nor merely an agent but both. One way in which this concept presents itself in Kant is in the term *humanity* that Kant introduces in the *Groundwork* and explains in the *Metaphysics of Morals*, as a being that has its own will in the sense of being able to set its own ends (G 4: 437; MM-DV 6: 387, 392). The fundamental principle of morality thus arises from reason's demand that *we not contradict the nature of human beings as rational agents, capable of setting their own ends*; an immoral maxim will thus have to be analyzed as one that commits a self-contradiction in both asserting and denying that one, some, or all human beings are such rational agents. But for the application of the law of noncontradiction to yield the kind of determinate result that morality expects it will have to start from the premise that *human beings are free agents.* That is the fact that cannot be contradicted. Kant's argument for the fundamental principle of morality will thus turn on the substantive claim that all human beings possess humanity, or are capable of setting their own ends. It will proceed by establishing that only universalizable maxims can avoid both asserting and denying the fact that human beings are free agents.

This is the argument we will analyze in this section. We can begin by establishing that the law of noncontradiction is indeed the first principle of reason on Kant's conception of reason. Kant does not explicitly mention the law of noncontradiction in his central arguments for the fundamental principle of morality, but he assumes it, and the relevance of what he does explicitly assert depends upon it. Kant does not need to make the principle itself explicit, for he works within a tradition that recognized the law of noncontradiction as the first principle of reason (and the principle of sufficient reason, which will come into his argument at a later stage, as the second). A fountainhead for this tradition was the philosophy of Gottfried Wilhelm Leibniz (1646–1716), and one of the sources for Leibniz's philosophy that was well-known in Kant's lifetime (much of Leibniz's work was published only after his death and Kant's as well) was the 1714 essay "The Monadology." Here Leibniz wrote:

> Our reasonings are based upon two great principles: the first the *principle of contradiction*, by virtue of which we judge that false which involves a contradiction, and that *true* which is opposed or contradictory to the false; and the second the *principle of sufficient reason*, by virtue of which we observe that there can be found no fact that is true or existent, or any true

> proposition, without there being a sufficient reason for its being so and not otherwise, although we cannot know these reasons in most cases.[36]

In the textbook that Kant used for his logic courses, influenced by the intervening logic texts of Christian Wolff (1679–1754) and Alexander Gottlieb Baumgarten (1714–1762), Georg Friedrich Meier (1718–1777), in a chapter titled "The Truth of Learned Cognition," wrote:

> The first internal characteristic of the truth of a cognition consists in its **inner possibility** insofar as it represents something possible and contains nothing contrary to itself, and also if one considers it totally by itself. . . . "The other internal characteristic of the truth of a cognition consists in its **being possible in a connection**. Consequently, (1) if it is a consequence of correct grounds, and (2) a ground of correct consequences. Accordingly, a cognition is true if it is not impossible and it is in conformity with the principle of sufficient ground.[37]

In the *Jäsche Logic*, the logic textbook published under Kant's name toward the end of his life, the first principle of logic is stated to be that "to the logical actuality of a cognition it pertains . . . **First**: that it be logically possible, i.e., **not contradict itself**" (JL, Introduction, section VII, 9: 51). Kant characterizes this as the first "of the universal laws of the understanding and of reason." Logic is the science of reason, broadly construed as the power of conceptualization, judgment, and inference, and the avoidance of contradiction is its first requirement and necessary condition for all others because the avoidance of contradiction is the necessary condition of truth itself. Kant makes the same point in the *Critique of Pure Reason*: "Whatever the content of our cognition may be, and however it may be related to the object, the general though to be sure only negative condition of all our judgments whatsoever is that they do not contradict themselves" (CPR A150/B189). In the first instance, this principle is the sufficient condition for the truth of *analytic* judgments, which simply make explicit the contents of concepts – contents that must not be self-contradictory if the concepts are to describe even logical possibilities; but although not a *sufficient* condition for all truth, the principle of noncontradiction is the first and *necessary* principle or criterion of *all* truth: "we must allow the **principle of contradiction** to count as the universal and completely sufficient **principle of all analytic cognition**; but its authority and usefulness does not extend beyond this, as a sufficient condition of truth. [But] that no cognition can be opposed to it without annihilating itself certainly makes this principle into a *conditio sine qua non*" of all truth, that is, its necessary condition

[36] "The Monadology," §§31–32; from Leibniz 1969, p. 646.
[37] Meier 2016, §§95–6, pp. 21–2.

(CPR A151-2/B191). For Kant, all truths that go beyond merely explicating the contents of a concept to assert some sort of fact will count as "synthetic" judgments (CPR A6-7/B10-11).[38]

Obviously the application of this condition or criterion for truth, whether as a sufficient condition for the truth of an analytic judgment or as a merely necessary condition for that of a synthetic judgment, always requires some concept that is to be determined to be free of internal or self-contradiction, or not, and then beyond that some true proposition that is not to be both affirmed and denied. There is no such thing as self-contradiction or freedom from self-contradiction as such; there are contradiction-free or self-contradictory concepts, or contradiction-free or self-contradictory applications of concepts to objects in judgments. Even in its first, merely negative form, the form of reason requires some matter to which it can be applied; beyond that, a concept that is free of *internal* contradiction must then be applied to something, of which it cannot then be denied: only then will an informative, synthetic judgment be made. And the fundamental principle of morality is surely supposed to be informative.

As the supreme principle of all analytic judgments, then, the law of noncontradiction must always have some concept to work with, but to yield any synthetic judgment it must also apply to some fact that cannot be both affirmed and denied. Let us see now how Kant derives the fundamental principle of morality from these simple premises. We have already encountered Kant's statement in the Preface to the *Groundwork* that the "ground of obligation" for all our duties must be sought "*a priori* simply in concepts of pure reason" (G 4: 389). At the outset of his central argument in Section II of the *Groundwork*, Kant says that moral laws and their fundamental principle must be derived "from the universal concept of a rational being as such" (G 4: 412). But as Kant's argument continues, it turns out that even the concept of a rational *being* is not specific enough to yield what he wants. What he needs is rather the concept of a rational *agent* as a being that has not merely the "capacity to determine itself to acting in conformity with the **representation of certain laws**" but that also determines itself to so act on a ground, namely an "end."[39]

[38] In the *Jäsche Logic*, Kant also refers to the law of excluded middle: "two contradicting judgments cannot both be true, and just as little can they both be false. If the one is true, then the other is false, and conversely" (§48, 9: 117). He does not usually refer to this principle in his main statements of the principles of reason, although perhaps his use of the principle of noncontradiction always assumes this principle. We will see one place where it might have been useful for him to make this principle explicit when we come later to the topic of collision of duties.

[39] Henry Allison thus correctly interprets the "different stages in the complete construction of the concept of the categorical imperative" as "correspond[ing] to stages in a progressive analysis of the concept of a finite rational agent" in Allison 2011, pp. 150–1.

That is, a rational agent determines itself to act in accordance with a law *for the sake of an end* (G 4: 426–7). Kant's argument will then be that the fundamental principle of morality can be derived from the application of the principle of noncontradiction to the concept of a rational agent as one capable of setting its own ends. This capacity must be affirmed of any rational agent and cannot be denied without contradiction. In the end to derive the *synthetic* proposition that the moral law *applies to us*, Kant will need to establish the fact that *we are* rational agents. But before we turn to that second step, let us see what form the first step of this argument takes in Kant's texts.

The capacity of a rational agent to set its own ends appears under different names in Kant's works. In the *Groundwork*, Kant assigns the name "humanity" to the "ground of a possible categorical imperative," although he makes it clear that this does not refer to a "**special property of human nature**" (G 4: 425), that is, to the biological fact of being a member of the species *Homo sapiens* or to any merely physiological or psychological trait characteristic of members of that species alone – it refers to the property of rational agency as present in human beings. Having begun his explication of the "ground of a possible categorical imperative" with the statement that "a human being and generally every rational being [*vernünftiges Wesen*] **exists** as an end in itself, **not merely as a means** for the discretionary use for this or that will" (G 4: 428), Kant concludes it with the formulation of the categorical imperative as "**So act that you use humanity, whether in your own person as well as in the person of any other, always at the same time as an end, never merely as a means**" (G 4: 429). In this most fundamental formulation of the categorical imperative Kant thus uses "humanity" to designate not what *distinguishes* human beings from other (possible) rational agents but rather *what they have in common*. And he then defines this, or more precisely "rational nature" (*vernünftige Natur*), as what makes a rational being into one, as "distinguished from the rest of nature by this, that it sets itself an end" (G 4: 437). Humanity is thus the capacity of human beings, like other rational agents (should there be any) but unlike the rest of nature, to set themselves ends. The same definition appears in the Introduction to the Doctrine of Virtue in the *Metaphysics of Morals* when Kant says that "humanity is that by which [a human being] alone is capable of setting himself ends" (section V.A, 6: 387) and "The capacity to set oneself an end – any end whatsoever – is what characterizes humanity (as distinct from animality)" (section VI.1, 6: 392).

But what Kant is referring to can also appear under the name of "will" (*Wille*) or as the power or faculty of "choice" (*Willkür*) once he has separated the former as the source of the moral law itself from the latter as the ability to choose whether or not to make the moral law one's own fundamental maxim, as he does in such works of the 1790s as *Religion within the Boundaries of Mere Reason* (6: 21, 23–4, 25, 31, 35, and more) and the *Metaphysics of Morals* (Introduction, 6: 226).[40] Thus our capacity to set our own ends appears under the name of the power of choice (*Willkür*) when Kant states his definition of "right" (*Recht*, or justice) as the "sum of the conditions under which the choice [*Willkür*] of one can be united with the choice of another in accordance with a universal law of freedom" and the "Universal Principle of Right" as "Every action is **right** if [in] it or in accordance with its maxim the freedom of choice [*Freiheit der Willkür*] of each can coexist with the freedom of everyone in accordance with a universal law" (MM-DR, Introduction, §§B and C, 6: 230).

The capacity to set our own ends can also appear without any special name at all in the guise of our ability to choose our own *maxims* of action, as in Kant's first and most common formulation of the categorical imperative as "**act only on such a maxim that you could at the same time will to become a universal law**" (G 4: 421), for to choose a maxim for acting is to choose an end and a means to realize it.[41] Thus all of these – humanity, the capacity of choice, the capacity to choose one's own maxims – are guises of the same thing: One exercises one's humanity by freely choosing a maxim, which sets an end to be reached by an action as the means thereto in the circumstances to which the maxim applies, or conversely, by choosing one's ends and adopting maxims about how to try to attain them. Kant also says that "rational being, as an end according to its nature," is the *matter* for the categorical imperative (G 4: 436); the fundamental principle of morality is then grounded in reason's application of its own *form* to this matter. In the passage in which he says this, he says that the form of a moral maxim consists in its "universality"; but, as we shall now see, that is a *consequence* of reason's most fundamental form, namely, its requirement of noncontradiction.

The foundational thought of Kant's moral philosophy is thus that this matter is will, choice, humanity – in a word, freedom – and that all human beings possess this. Thus in our intentional actions, in Kant's terminology in our adoption of maxims for actions, we must – insofar as we are to be rational – avoid contradicting the fact that we and anyone else potentially affected by our

[40] At MM 6: 227, Kant might seem to deny what he has asserted in Rel when he states that "freedom of choice [*Freiheit der Willkür*] *cannot* be defined as the ability to make a choice [*Vermögen der Wahl*] to act for or against the law (*libertas indifferentiae*)" (emphasis added). I have argued that what he means is that this cannot be the "real definition" of freedom, which must include its *ratio cognoscendi*, which is our ability to choose to act *for* the moral law, but that once we have come to know that we have the freedom to choose for the moral law it also follows that we could choose to act *against* it as well. See Guyer 2018, pp. 133–7.

[41] For analyses of Kant's concept of maxims along these lines see O'Neill 2013, ch. 3, especially pp. 97–103, and Korsgaard 1989, especially pp. 57–8.

actions *have wills, possess humanity, in short, are free*. This idea is clear in a note in his own copy of his 1764 book *Observations on the Feeling of the Beautiful and Sublime*, among Kant's earliest recorded remarks on morality. Kant first suggests that morality is grounded on the psychological fact of our abhorrence of domination by others: "what is harder and more unnatural than [the] yoke of necessity" from the harshness of nature "is the subjection of one human being under the will of another. No misfortune can be more terrifying to one who is accustomed to freedom . . . than to see himself delivered to a creature of his own kind who can compel him to do what he will (to give himself over to his will" (Kant 2005, p. 11). This describes a feeling of aversion to constraint by others that can be assumed to be widely shared among human beings under normal circumstances. When he wrote this Kant was still attracted to the moral sense theory of Anthony Ashley Cooper, the third Earl of Shaftesbury (1671–1714), and Francis Hutcheson (1692–1746) and was at least willing to consider that the fundamental principle of morality could be grounded on a widely shared feeling.[42]

But the same note also suggests a logical rather than merely psychological foundation for morality, in the form of the thought that what makes domination immoral is that it is equivalent to or assumes a self-contradictory assertion that *a being with its own will does not have such a will*: "There is in subjection not only something externally dangerous but also a certain ugliness and a contradiction that at the same time indicates its injustice . . . that a human being should as it were need no soul himself and have no will of his own, and that another soul should move my limbs, is absurd and perverse" (Kant 2005, p. 12). "Ugliness" and "perverse" may be psychological terms, implying a feeling of aversion toward constraint; but "contradiction" and "absurd" are logical terms, the former obviously so, implying that there is a violation of logic and not just of feeling in such treatment – although a violation of logic may be accompanied by a feeling of aversion, just as Kant will later argue that consciousness of the moral law is accompanied by or even takes the form of a feeling of respect that is a phenomenological mixture of pain and pleasure (G 4: 401-2n, CPrR 5: 73–6). Thus it is not just psychologically repulsive but also logically contradictory to assert that a being with a will of its own does not have such a will. Strictly speaking, it is judgments or propositions that can be self-contradictory or not, not actions as such, but Kant must be assuming that to act in a way that denies the freedom of another entails a judgment denying that the other has her own will even when the agent must also accept the judgment

[42] In Kant 1993, see *Inquiry Concerning the Distinctness of the Principles of Natural Theology and Morals* (1764), 2:273–301, at 2:300, and "M. Immanuel Kant's Announcement of the Program of his Lectures for the Winter Semester 1765–1766," 2:303–13, at 2:311–12.

that she does, and thus entails a proper self-contradiction.[43] The first rule of morality is thus that this contradiction be avoided: Logic itself forbids us to treat a being with a will of its own as one that does not have a will of its own.

In this early note, Kant applies the principle of noncontradiction to other-regarding actions and to the judgments that they implicitly involve: One must not treat another being that has a will of its own, the ability to set its own ends, as if it did not have its own will. But a violation of self-regarding duty, in Kant's language duty to self, would similarly consist in allowing one's own free choice to be dominated by one's mere impulses or inclinations, and Kant treats this as if this were a willful denial that one has a free will oneself, when one knows perfectly well that one does. Thus in our next evidence of Kant's developing moral philosophy, Kant's lectures on ethics from the mid-1770s,[44] the idea that a violation of duty is a violation of the law of noncontradiction is explicit in Kant's treatment of duties to self. Here, again referring to actions rather than judgments, Kant formulates the fundamental principle of morality as the requirement of *self-consistency* in the use of one's freedom or "powers," in the first instance in the use of it in acts affecting one's own continuing use of freedom, or of compatibility between each use of one's own freedom and the "greatest use" of one's freedom, the possibility of its use in all the other cases in which one might use it; but again he must be assuming that inconsistency in action commits one to self-contradictory assertions. He first puts the point by saying that since the use of freedom without any rule is a person's "greatest misfortune ... it has to be restricted, not, though, by other properties and faculties, but by itself"; that is, our use of freedom on multiple occasions has to be internally consistent rather than contradictory. Kant then formulates the fundamental principle of morality, in its application to self-regarding actions: "Its supreme rule is: In all self-regarding actions, so to behave that any use of powers is compatible with the greatest use of them." This is a requirement of self-consistency or the avoidance of contradiction in the exercise of one's freedom: "Only under certain conditions can freedom be consistent with itself; otherwise it comes into collision with itself." For example, "if I have drunk too much today, I am incapable of making use of my freedom and my powers; or if I do away with myself, I likewise deprive myself of the ability to use them" (Eth-C 27: 346). That is, drinking too much or committing suicide, considered

[43] Again, see Piper 1997 and Piper 2013, volume II.

[44] The text that has been translated into English twice and is generally cited is known as "Moral Philosophy Collins" and is dated 1784–5. But it is virtually identical to a text known as *Moralphilosophie Kaehler* from the summer semester of 1777 (Kant 2004), so Collins, a student who matriculated in 1783, must have copied his notes from an older text similar to Kaehler's.

by themselves, in isolation from our other possible actions, are free acts, but they are free acts temporarily or permanently incompatible with the possibility of further free acts, free uses of one's powers. They are in fact actions that would undermine or destroy one's longer-term possession of freedom. Kant takes such acts as ones that would both assert and deny one's own freedom, while reason demands the avoidance of such self-contradiction. Kant puts the point in similar terms in a note contemporaneous with these lectures: "No intention can take place contrary to . . . the essential determinations of one's own person and of life itself," where "essential determinations are those without which one would either not be a human being or a free being" (Refl 6801, 19:165; 1772–5? 1772?). As one commentator explains, "it is a contradiction to acknowledge oneself as a free rational being and yet on the basis of this reason to annihilate the usability of reason through suicide."[45]

Kant does not explicitly talk about self-consistency in the use of freedom or the self-contradiction in denying our freedom in the *Groundwork* itself. But one line in the lectures does point toward Kant's subsequent terminology: A few pages before the previous citations, he says that "[i]t is utterly absurd that a rational being, who is an end whereto every means exists, should use himself as a means" (Eth-C 27: 343). "Absurd" here translates *widersinnig*, which is not the same word Kant had used in the note in his copy of the *Observations* a decade earlier – that was *ungereimt* – but if anything it brings out even more clearly the logical rather than psychological character of Kant's point: It contradicts the unavoidable application of the concept of a person as a rational being and hence as an end to any human being to treat it merely as a means. Kant treats this as a self-contradiction and thus a violation of the first principle of reason.

Another revealing comment is found in Kant's course on "natural right" from the summer semester of 1784 – just when Kant was writing the *Groundwork*. Here Kant says that "a rational being is never a mere means, [but is] instead at the same time an end," and then "[a] human being is an end so it is contradictory to say that a human being should be a mere means . . . For every human being is himself an end and thus he cannot be a mere means." Kant further states that "The inner value of a human being is based on his freedom, that he has a will of its own"; the contradiction in treating a human being, whether oneself or another, as a mere means to an end rather than as an end in itself would be the self-contradiction of asserting that something that does have freedom or a will of its own does not. Kant makes clear that we do use people as means to our own ends all the time: When I contract with a mason to build a house or hire a servant, I am using that person as a means to some end of my own; but if

[45] Busch 1979, p. 79.

I am to do this *morally*, then the arrangement must also serve some end of the other, in virtue of which "[h]e must also will it" and can therefore "consent" to it (L-NR 27: 1319). Here Kant explicitly characterizes the moral failure of treating anyone as a mere means rather than as an end as a logical failure, the assertion of a contradiction.

The thought underlying these earlier passages, I propose, underlies Kant's second main formulation of the categorical imperative in the *Groundwork*, the Formula of Humanity: "**So act that you use humanity, whether in your own person or the person of any other, always at the same time as an end, never merely as a means**" (G 4: 429). For if humanity is the capacity of a being to set its own ends, then one must never use one's own capacity to set ends in a way that treats the capacity to set ends, whether in oneself or in anyone and everyone else, merely as a means – which is the same as always to use it as an end. Thus in setting one's own end on a single occasion one must not treat one's own future freedom merely as means to one's present end, and one must treat others not merely as means to one's own ends but also as beings able to set *their* own ends, whose capacity to do so is not impaired by one's own freely chosen actions. Only this, in Kant's view, will satisfy reason's first principle of noncontradiction with regard to the undeniable fact of one's own and others' agency.

Other features of Kant's language in the *Groundwork* show that, as in his lectures, he thinks that treating any person merely as a means rather than as an end contradicts his or her "essential determinations." Kant explains his assertion of the Formula of Humanity thus:

> [R]ational beings are called **persons** because *their nature already marks them out* as an end in itself, that is, as something that may not be used merely as a means, and hence so far limits all choice . . . These, therefore, are not merely subjective ends, the existence of which as an effect of our action has a worth **for us**, but rather **objective ends**, that is, beings the existence of which is in itself an end. (G 4: 428, italics added)

Kant also talks about our *nature* as the basis of morality in his final formulation of the categorical imperative, the formula that "[m]orality consists . . . in the reference of all actions to the lawgiving by which alone a realm of ends is possible" (G 4: 434), when he states that every rational being is "fit to be a member of a possible realm of ends" because "he was already destined to be [so] *by his own nature* as an end in itself" (G 4: 435, italics added). Again, his idea is that it is a fact that a person, any person, is an end, so it is (or implies) a contradiction to act toward any person as if she were not, and contradictions must be avoided. The form of reason requires in the first instance the avoidance of contradiction; the matter for reason is that persons are ends. If persons are ends because they set ends, and that is the same as exercising their freedom, then the fact for reason is that persons are free, and the form of reason requires that their freedom not be contradicted.

The necessity of avoiding this contradiction in how we think about ourselves and others as persons underlies the necessity of avoiding the kind of contradiction that Kant more explicitly discusses in the *Groundwork*, namely the contradiction between the maxim of action that an agent is considering adopting[46] and the universalization of that maxim, for it is only the necessity of avoiding the underlying contradiction in how we think of persons as free agents that requires us to consider the consequences of universalizing our maxims in the first place. The contradiction between our maxims and their universalization that we need to avoid can take two forms. First, there is the contradiction that arises when "Some actions are so constituted that their maxim cannot even be **thought** without contradiction as a universal law of nature," or what is often called the "contradiction in conception" of an immoral action. Second, there is the "contradiction in willing" that arises when the universalization of one's proposed maxim does not seem to contradict acting on that maxim considered in isolation, but conflicts with some more general feature of rational willing. We have to ask these questions about the consequences of the universalization of our maxims just because we have to apply the law of noncontradiction to the fact that we ourselves and others are all free agents and thus any maxim on which we propose to act cannot contradict that fact. This is why I have to ask whether acting on my proposed maxim now would contradict my own freedom or ability to will more generally, thus being able to exercise my freedom on any future occasion on which I could otherwise do so, and why I have to ask whether my acting on my proposed maxim would contradict the freedom of all others to act on maxims of their own choice, including the same maxim I propose to act upon if they so choose. Assuming that I must recognize or affirm the fact of my own freedom and that of others, I can act rationally only on maxims that are consistent with my own future freedom and likewise with the freedom of all others. To do otherwise would be to deny the freedom of some agent or agents that cannot be denied, or to commit a self-contradiction. Thus Kant's requirement of universalizability follows from the formula of humanity and is ultimately grounded in the law of noncontradiction because the latter is. Avoidance of any contradiction between a maxim and its universalization is itself required by the underlying requirement to avoid contradicting the nature of agents as free wills.

[46] This is an idealization; it is not part of Kant's theory that a moral agent must be consciously performing the universalization tests to be described at the time of acting. The requirement is only that the maxim that would explain her action could pass the tests.

The requirement to avoid contradiction between one's maxim and its universalization depends upon the requirement to avoid contradiction between one exercise of freedom and other exercises of freedom, whether one's own possible future exercises of freedom or those of others.

We can see this in Kant's illustration of the application of the requirement that our maxims also be universalizable (the Formula of Universal Law) in Section I of the *Groundwork*. Faced with a situation in which a lying promise – one that I make with no intention of keeping – could get me out of some difficulties, Kant says,

> I ask myself: would I indeed be content that my maxim (to get myself out of difficulties by a false promise) should hold as a universal law (for myself as well as others)? . . . I soon become aware that I could indeed will the lie, but by no means a universal law to lie; for in accordance with such a law there would properly be no promises at all, since it would be futile to avow my will with regard to my future actions to others who would not believe this avowal . . . and thus my maxim, as soon as it were made a universal law, would have to destroy itself. (G 4: 403)

In a world in which everyone tried to make false promises, no one would accept any promises, so I could not make a false promise after all. Morality does not ask me to believe that my making one false promise would actually cause everyone else to try to do so on every occasion as well and thus bring the whole practice of promising tumbling down. But it does ask me to imagine how it would be *if* everyone were to act on the maxim on which I propose to act, because morality requires me to act on a maxim *only if* it *could* also be a universal law.[47] Thus, morality requires me to avoid a contradiction between the maxim on which I would act and the universalization of that maxim. But why does morality require me to ask whether my maxim could be universalized? If "the ground of a possible categorical imperative" (G 4: 428) is that its nature marks out every person as an end in itself, it is because this is necessary to avoid contradicting the nature of persons, oneself and all others potentially affected by one's own adoption of the maxim, potentially all others period. The necessity of avoiding contradiction between a proposed maxim and its universalization is a consequence of the necessity of avoiding contradicting the nature of rational beings as persons with free will.

In Section II of the *Groundwork*, Kant illustrates both the Formula of Universal Law and the Formula of Humanity with examples of duties derivable

[47] Onora O'Neill interprets the categorical imperative as asking whether acting on a maxim would be consistent with its "universalized typified counterpart" in O'Neill 2013, p. 140; Rawls describes the test as whether it would be possible to act on the maxim in the "adjusted social world" in which it is universalized; see Rawls 2000, "Kant II," p. 169.

from them.[48] He uses a common distinction between perfect and imperfect duties (G 4: 421n.), which he later explains as the difference between duties to perform or refrain from specific actions in specific circumstances, and duties to adopt certain general ends, which leave open how and in what circumstances one can best realize them (MM-DV, Introduction, section II, 6: 382–3). He then maps this distinction onto that between duties to oneself and duties to others, so that there are four classes of duties, and offers one example of each class. His example of a perfect duty to self is the duty not to commit suicide, that of a perfect duty to others is the duty not to make false promises (as in Section I), that of an imperfect duty to self is the duty to cultivate one's potential talents, and an imperfect duties to others is the duty of beneficence, or the duty to assist others in need (G 4: 421–3 and 429–30). The examples of perfect duties are supposed to show that there would be a contradiction in willing both a particular maxim and its universalization; the examples of imperfect duty are supposed to show that the universalization of the maxim in question would contradict some more general principle of the rational will that the agent cannot deny himself or others to have. Kant thus describes the first two cases as ones in which proposed "actions are so constituted that their maxim cannot even be *thought* without contradiction as a universal law of nature," while in the two cases of imperfect duties "that inner impossibility is indeed not to be found, but it is still impossible to *will* that their maxim be raised to the universality of a law of nature because such a will would contradict itself" (G 4: 424). In all cases, the impossibility of rationally *acting* upon the maxim under consideration is supposed to follow from the logical contradiction that would arise between the proposition describing action upon the maxim and the proposition describing the consequences of the universalization of the maxim; the "practical contradiction" in attempting to act upon the maxim thus follows from that straightforward logical contradiction.[49]

[48] Allen Wood has pointed out that at G 4: 423–4 the 1785 and 1786 editions of the *Groundwork* print refer to an *Abteilung* rather than *Ableitung* of duties, that is, to a fourfold *classification* or "division" of duties rather than to a *derivation* of four examples of duties from the first formulation of the categorical imperative; see Wood 2017, pp. 26–7n, and inferred from this that Kant does not intend to derive duties from the categorical imperative by anything like the categorical imperative "procedure" of which interpreters such as O'Neill and Rawls speak. This claim is belied by Kant's prefatory statement that once having proceeded "analytically from common cognition to the determination of its supreme [moral] principle," the *Groundwork* will in turn proceed "synthetically from the examination of this principle and its sources back to the common cognition in which we find it used" (G 4: 392), which suggests that Kant believes he can *deduce* (synthetically) the commonly recognized (classes of) duties from his formulation(s) of the moral law.

[49] I thus agree with Adrian Piper in rejecting Christine Korsgaard's view that there is a distinct category of "practical contradiction" in Kant. See Korsgaard 1986, Piper 2012, p. 253, and Piper 2018, p. 2041.

Kant's application of the universalizability requirement for moral maxims works better in some of his examples than others, but in all his cases the underlying contradiction between the consequences of one free act and the fact of the freedom of all parties concerned, which is prohibited by the Formula of Humanity, is clear. Thus Kant's first explanation of the immorality of committing suicide in order, out of self-love, to avoid future pain, is that a law of nature that is supposed "to impel toward the furtherance of life would contradict itself and would therefore not subsist as" a law of nature (G 4: 422); but the problem here arises not from the potential universalization of the would-be suicide's maxim, but from Kant's supposition that a proper law could not have one outcome in one set of circumstances and the opposite one in another, which is palpably false. But Kant's subsequent explanation that a person who would commit suicide is not treating himself as an end because "in order to escape from a trying condition he makes use of [his own] person **merely as a means** to maintain a tolerable condition up to the end of his life" (G 4: 429) involves no such mistake, but simply assumes that there is a contradiction in treating an end as if it were merely a means, namely that of treating a free agent as if it were not a free agent, more precisely treating a free agent now as if it would not otherwise continue to be a free agent. The real nature of the contradiction that must be avoided is even clearer in Kant's treatment of suicide in his lectures, when he says that the problem is that in committing that act "a person uses his freedom to destroy himself . . . the person is here employing his powers and freedom against himself, to make himself a carcass," that is, he is using his freedom against his (continued) freedom (Eth-C 27: 343). Kant's second example, the perfect duty to others not to make false or fraudulent promises to them, works better as an example of both the Formula of Universal Law and that of Humanity. In the first case, Kant's argument is that if one's intended maxim of making a false promise to get a loan were universalized, no one would believe and accept promises, so one's own maxim would be contradicted by its universalization; specifically, the consequences of the universalization of the maxim of false promising would contradict the very possibility of the promise one intends to make, thus "it would make the promise and the end one might have in it itself impossible" (G 4: 422). After stating the Formula of Humanity, Kant explains the problem with a false promise as that it would "make use of another human being **merely as a means**" for the other "cannot possibly agree to my way of behaving toward him" (G 4: 429–30). My use of my own freedom in making a false promise would not be compatible with the freedom of the victim of my promise. But since the other *is* free, and I know this, to treat him in this way would be to contradict myself; and it is because insofar as I am rational I must not commit such a contradiction that I must always ask whether my proposed maxim would treat everyone potentially affected by it as free, that is, ask whether my maxim is also universalizable.

Kant presents his two examples of imperfect duty, the duty to cultivate one's own potential talents and the duty to be helpful to others, as if their universalization does not involve an outright contradiction but only some more general failure of rational willing, and thus would seem to justify the interpretation that he needs a special category of "practical" contradiction in addition to logical contradiction. Thus in his treatment of the duty not to let one's talents rust under the Formula of Universal Law he says that an agent who would do so fails to see that developing his talents could "serve him ... for all sorts of possible purposes" and thus fails to have a rational will (G 4: 423), while following the Formula of Humanity he says that both developing one's talents and helping others are necessary to treat oneself and others fully or positively as ends in themselves, not merely as means to something else (G 4: 430). But Kant's first treatment of the duty to help makes clear that this duty can be derived from the requirement of universalizability: A will that would adopt the maxim never to help others would, *if it universalized this maxim*, "conflict with itself, since many cases would occur in which one would need the love and sympathy of others and in which, by such a law of nature arisen from his own will, he would rob himself of all hope of the assistance he wishes for himself" (G 4: 423; he similarly says in the *Metaphysics of Morals* that "I want everyone else to be benevolent to me; hence I ought also to be benevolent toward everyone else"; MM-DV, §27, 6: 451, see also §30, 6: 453). That is, such a person has to be supposed as both willing that he be able to obtain help from others when he needs it yet willing that no one help anyone else when they need it, which is a contradiction. Or perhaps more deeply, such a person would be taking a contradictory stance toward himself: he would be asserting that he never needs help from others, but at the same time cannot avoid willing to have help from others when he needs it, for only thus can he really treat himself as an end; and he has to universalize the maxim of getting help from others when he needs it into the maxim of helping others when they need it because only thus can he treat them as ends. A similar argument would underlie the duty to cultivate one's own talents: One could will, or pretend to will, to let one's talents rust, but as a free and rational agent one must also will that one have the means to one's ends, even if one has the end of merely lying idle, and having those means available (given that our ancestors were expelled from the Garden of Eden and someone has to work) will mean that someone, oneself or others, must have developed their talents – and if one is to treat all as equally free, one cannot just will that others develop their talents without doing so oneself. Both the arguments about how one must treat oneself and how one must treat others depend on the underlying claim that humanity in oneself and others – that is, the freedom of oneself and others – must not be contradicted.

It might be objected that the arguments for the imperfect duties depend upon an additional premise about rationality, namely that one cannot rationally will an end without having, or believing oneself to have, some sufficient means to that end, and this is not a matter of mere logic, thus that at least in these cases Kant does after all need a special notion of the practical contradiction that a rational will must avoid beyond the ordinary notion of logical contradiction. Kant maintains, however, that the principle "Whoever wills the end also wills (insofar as reason has decisive influence on his actions) the indispensably necessary means to it that are within his power" is, "as regards the volition, analytic" (G 4: 417). That is, he supposes that it is part of the concept of willing, as opposed to that of mere wishing, that one take oneself to have and will to use adequate means to the end that one wills, and conversely that it is also part of the concept of willing that you cannot will an end to which you do not have means. Thus it is a logical contradiction to will an end but not will the means; it is therefore a contradiction to conceive of yourself as a being who is free to will all sorts of ends – *as you must* – yet not will to provide means by cultivating your talents, and likewise it is a contradiction to conceive of others as beings who are free to will all sorts of ends – *as you must* – yet not will to help provide them with means to their ends. Voluntarily to deny oneself or others means that one could provide is to deny oneself or others the ability to rationally will the ends that would depend on those means, and in Kant's view that would be to contradict the nature of oneself and others as free agents who can set themselves all sorts of ends.

Arthur Schopenhauer (1788–1860), who modeled his theoretical philosophy on Kant's, charged that Kant's moral philosophy is a sham because the reasoning that I have just described is actually *instrumental* reasoning, not "pure" practical reasoning.[50] His objection is that the supposed moral agent is really considering only the consequences for his own action, ultimately for his own happiness, when he asks whether he could still act on his maxim or will more generally in the face of the universalization of his maxim. In his view, the Kantian agent is only asking himself whether he could still get away with his fraudulent promise if everyone made such promises or whether he could still successfully pursue his own goals in general if no one else were to help him. We have just seen part of what should be Kant's response to this objection, namely that the principle that you can only will an end if you can will the means is

[50] See Schopenhauer 2010, vol. I, p. 556, and Schopenhauer 2009, pp. 155–9.

a matter of logic, following from the concept of willing itself, not a mere matter of prudence. But, even more important, Kant does not require that you consider the universalization of your maxim as a matter of personal prudence, although instrumental reasoning comes in when you figure out what the consequences of that universalization would be. For it is morality, not mere prudence, that requires you to ask whether you could act on your maxim if *everyone* acted on that maxim, the question that you must ask in order not to deny that anyone who has a will does have one. Prudence requires you to consider whether others would *actually* adopt your maxim if you set the example for them, and if so, how many – enough to get in the way of your action, or not that many, so you might still get away with it? But morality does not ask that question; morality simply asks what would happen *if* everyone adopted your maxim, because morality insists that you not deny the freedom of anyone who is in fact free, including their freedom to adopt the same maxim that you do. You have to consider the consequences of the universalization of your maxim in order to see whether there is a contradiction lurking in it, but you have to universalize your maxim in the first place simply in order not to contradict the fact that all persons are themselves free agents or possess humanity.[51]

One might also object to Kant's assumption that *acting* in a certain way commits one to the *assertion* of certain propositions, for self-contradiction is in the first instance a property of propositions in virtue of the concepts included in them, and this might seem problematic. The practical use of reason, however, does presuppose its theoretical use. That is, although it would be ludicrous to insist that performing an action necessarily involves actually uttering the propositions that express the facts presupposed by the rationality of the action – just as it would be ludicrous to suppose that a rational agent must consciously consider or utter the maxim or principle on which she is acting at the moment of action – rational beings do act within a framework of theoretical beliefs as well as practical principles, and their actions will be irrational if the set of beliefs that underlie those actions is self-contradictory or incoherent, just as they will be irrational if their maxims are self-contradictory. In Kant's terms, "a rational being has the capacity to act **in accordance with the representation of laws**, that is, in accordance with principles . . . **reason** is required for the derivation of

[51] Thus David Cummiskey was correct to argue that Kant's moral philosophy *entails* a "consequentialist normative theory . . . that requires the promotion of the good" (in his words, that the latter can be "derived" from the former), but wrong to suppose that this "undermines" Kantian deontology: that we must promote our own good and that of others follows from the fact that we must recognize and not contradict the fact that we ourselves and all others possess humanity or are free to set ends. See Cummiskey 1996, p. 88.

actions from laws" (G 4: 412).[52] A rational being – more precisely a being capable of rationality insofar as it is acting rationally, not, for example, merely slipping or falling – does not simply move without some beliefs about what it is doing; it acts on the basis of a belief that acting in that way is the way to bring about some state of affairs that it wants to bring about but also on the basis of beliefs about what its circumstances are, including what kinds of object surround it, and if there is something incoherent or self-contradictory in its presuppositions – for example, that the objects around it do not possess humanity, when they do – then, again insofar as it is rational, it will not act that way. A rational being avoids contradiction in the beliefs presupposed by its principles as much as it avoids contradiction in its principles, and on the argument I have been attributing to Kant its principles depend on certain beliefs, above all the belief that both itself and the other persons with whom it may interact have their own wills.

But surely another question has been nagging at the reader throughout this section: How can Kant take it for granted that each of us knows that everyone possesses humanity in the sense of the capacity to set his or her own ends? How can I know this about others? Indeed, how can I even know it about myself? Kant himself suggests that this is an unresolved question in a footnote to his argument for the assertion that "the human being and in general every rational being **exists** as an end in itself, **not merely as a means** to be used by this or that will at its discretion" (G 4:428). His argument is that "[t]he human being necessarily represents his own existence in this way; so far it is thus a **subjective** principle of human actions. But every other rational being also represents his existence in this way consequent on just the same rational ground that also holds for me;* thus it is at the same an **objective** principle from which, as a supreme practical ground, it must be possible to derive all laws of the will" (G 4: 429). At the asterisk, thus to the assertion that there is an objective ground for treating every rational being as an end in itself and not merely as a means to the ends of some other being, Kant then notes: "Here I put this proposition forward as a postulate. The grounds for it will be found in the last section" (G 4: 429n). This is a tantalizing suggestion that Kant will subsequently prove what he is here merely assuming. But Kant does not reintroduce the term "postulate" in the final section of the *Groundwork* to which he is referring, so it is not immediately obvious how he thinks he is redeeming this promissory note there. Examination

[52] Kant continues this sentence by saying that since reason is required for the derivation of actions from laws, "the will is nothing other than practical reason." But that actually holds only for completely rational beings, which we human beings are not; as Kant will eventually make clear, above all in *Religion within the Boundaries of Mere Reason*, the human will can will contrary to reason – that is what makes evil possible.

of the central argument of Section III, however, will show that Kant is attempting to prove the fact that we have free wills, the fact to which the principle of noncontradiction can be applied.

A self-contradiction arises only when the same predicate is both asserted and denied *of the same object, at the same time* (see CPR A32/B48-9), so it has to be shown that the predicate that Kant takes to be denied when someone, oneself or anyone else, is treated merely as a means, namely that such a person has a will of its own, *in fact has to be asserted both of oneself and everyone else*. Further, since it is not a contradiction merely to assert something false about an object, whether out of ignorance or malice, but is a contradiction only to *both* assert and deny the same predicate of an object, the moral agent – *any* moral agent, anyone to whom the moral law is to be self-evident, that is, any of us – must *know* that we are all beings with free wills if that agent is to be guilty of self-contradiction in acting toward any moral subject as if he or she did not have her own will. Kant's central argument in Section III of the *Groundwork* can then be read as an attempt to discharge precisely this burden of proof. Kant does not want merely to *presuppose* that the positive concept of freedom, or of "autonomy, that is, the will's property of being a law to itself" (G 4: 446–7) applies to us all; that would run the risk that we are merely trapped in a circle of concepts linking the concept of freedom with that of the moral law but are begging the question whether we really are free (G 4: 450). The fact of our freedom has to be proven, not merely presupposed, and in a way that shows that *everyone of us really knows this*: Only then will it follow that we violate the law of noncontradiction if we act toward any person, ourself or anyone else, as if they did not have their own will but were mere means to ours, for only then would we be asserting to be false something that we cannot but know to be true.

Kant's claim is that at the deepest level of our being we are self-active and rational, able to set our own ends but also to do so in accordance with the law that reason gives itself – in other words, the universal principle of morality – which is, however, nothing but the law not to treat anyone, ourselves or others, in a way that denies our freedom. His argument appeals to his doctrine of transcendental idealism, that is, his view that there is a fundamental difference between the way that things appear to us and the way that they are in themselves, specifically, that space, time, and our ordinary model of causation of temporally successive effects by temporally antecedent causes apply to the way things appear to us but not to things as themselves.[53] In spite of having taken the entire *Critique of Pure Reason* to establish this doctrine, Kant says in the *Groundwork*

[53] For my interpretation and critique of Kant's transcendental idealism, see Guyer 1987, Part V, and Guyer 2017. For a different interpretation and a defense of Kant's theory, see Allison 2004.

that "no subtle reflection" is required to make this distinction and that even the "commonest understanding" makes it as soon as it reflects on the difference between the effects of external objects on our senses and those objects themselves (G 4: 451). He then says that "[e]ven as to himself, the human being" – again, any human being – "cannot claim to cognize what he is in himself through the cognizance he has by inner sensation," but rather "beyond this constitution of his own subject, made up of nothing but appearances, he must necessarily assume something else lying at their basis, namely his I as it may be constituted in itself." Thus, Kant continues, "as regards mere perception and receptivity to sensations" the human being "must count himself as belonging to the **world of sense**, but with regard to what there may be of pure activity in him . . . he must count himself as belonging to the **intellectual world**, which however he does not further know" (G 4: 451). Kant places more weight on the "pure activity" of the self as it is in itself than on the disclaimer of further knowledge of that self, however, for in the next stage of the argument he insists that reason is not merely what distinguishes us from the rest of the objects *within* nature but also *from ourselves* as mere objects in nature; thus reason is what is characteristic of us as we are *in ourselves*, and that reason is "pure self-activity," a "spontaneity so pure that it goes beyond anything that sensibility can ever afford" (G 4: 452). Since we cannot but recognize the truth of the distinction between our apparent and real selves, and cannot doubt our essential freedom at the latter level, to deny that we have free wills would actually be to assert a self-contradiction.

Kant's argument seems deeply problematic. One objection I will *not* raise is that Kant is attempting to derive an "ought" from an "is," that is, a fundamental normative principle from a fundamental factual principle. That is precisely what Kant is doing – namely, arguing that we must treat persons *as* ends in themselves because it would contradict their nature as free agents to treat them as mere means to something else. That is how the "postulate" that persons are ends in themselves is to be proved.[54] The objections I will raise, however, are these. First, it seems to violate the epistemological restriction of transcendental idealism as expounded in the first *Critique*, namely that all we can know of things in themselves, *any* things in themselves, is that they exist but that they are not spatiotemporal (e.g., CPR A26/B42).[55] Second, even if Kant's argument were

[54] It is a myth that David Hume proved that an ought cannot be derived from an is; what he actually argued was rather that oughts must be derived from the *right* facts, namely facts about our moral sentiments. Kant disagreed with the latter, but not with the more general strategy that "ought" may be derived from the right "is." See Guyer 2009b.

[55] I have criticized the argument of *Groundwork* III on this ground in Guyer 2007a, pp. 150–62, Guyer 2007b, and Guyer 2009a. Julian Wuerth has defended it on the ground that Kant's argument that we cannot know things in themselves applies to objects acting upon us, not to our own mental actions; see Wuerth 2014, pp. 321–4.

sound, it looks like an argument that each one of us could make *only in his or her own case*, thus one by which each of us could prove *him- or herself* free, but not one by which each of us could prove that *everyone else is free*, which would be required if acting toward *others* as if they were mere means to our own wills and not wills in their own right is to entail a self-contradiction.[56]

Kant may not have raised the latter objection himself because he generally believes that we have no other way to think about other people than the way in which we think about ourselves, and no particular reason to think there is anything dubious about so thinking of them – Kant is no fan of generalized or "Cartesian" skepticism.[57] About the former objection, that Kant's claim that we all know that our real essence or "authentic self" (G 4: 57) is free, self-active will violates the strictures of transcendental idealism, maybe the problem is with transcendental idealism rather than the claim that we know that we are all beings with our own wills, however exactly we understand what it is to have a will. In any case, as our quotation from Kant's early note that it is "absurd" and a "contradiction" to act toward a being that has a will of its own as if it did not shows, his commitment to this thought long preceded his development of the epistemology of transcendental idealism and the metaphysics of freedom of the will within transcendental idealism and it retained its grip on him in spite of this doctrine. Maybe it should grip us as well in spite of this doctrine.

Kant himself must have had qualms about his direct assertion of the self-activity of reason, for in the *Critique of Practical Reason* he instead proceeds from our supposedly immediate consciousness of the moral law as a "fact of reason" to the further inference that we have a "pure" or free will – which would then also be a fact. But this argument too presupposes transcendental idealism as the condition of the possibility of freedom as an alternative to the thoroughgoing causation that we observe throughout the empirical world (CPrR 5: 29–30), and is still subject to the objection that it is an argument that anyone could use to prove her *own* freedom from her *own* consciousness of the moral law, but not an argument by means of which one person could prove that *everyone else* has free will. So Kant's shift in strategy does not automatically escape the problems of his theory of free will in the face of his transcendental idealism and the problems of transcendental idealism itself. And perhaps we should not worry overmuch about these issues, because we might be able to apply Kant's more general strategy for the derivation of the moral law to the empirical fact that normal mature human beings do have the capacity to set their own ends, however that is to be understood metaphysically and whether it implies everything someone might want from a concept of free will.

[56] For this objection, see Guyer 2008b. [57] See Guyer 2003 and Forster 2008.

Be all that as it may, we must now turn to the next stage of Kant's account of the rationality of morality, namely his application of the second fundamental principle of reason in general, the principle of sufficient reason, to the case of human action.

4 The Principle of Sufficient Reason and the Idea of the Highest Good

Kant insisted that happiness alone could never be the ground of the fundamental principle of morality or the goal of morally worthy action. Nevertheless, he recognized that happiness is a natural goal of human beings, indeed, as the sum of the satisfaction of their individual desires, the natural goal for human beings, and that a place has to be found for it in morality. He found that place in the form of the "highest good," the "complete object" of morality that combines happiness with virtue as the worthiness to be happy. Reason's second principle, the principle of sufficient reason, plays a central role in Kant's argument that the highest good is the complete object of morality.

The principle of sufficient reason is the principle that for every fact there is a sufficient reason – that is, an adequate ground or explanation. In the hands of traditional metaphysicians such as Leibniz, this principle quickly led to a proof of the existence of God as the complete explanation of all other facts taken together, while any possible infinite regress of reasons could be stopped by a conception of God as, in the terms of Baruch Spinoza (1632–77), a *causa sui* or cause of himself. Kant rejected all such uses of the principle in what he called "speculative" metaphysics as outstripping the limits of our sensibility and thus the possibility of confirmation, and confined the use of the principle in theoretical philosophy to causal explanation within the limits of experience (see CPR A200-1/B246). But our conception of what *ought* to be in moral philosophy is not constrained by the limits of what we can know to be through the senses, and here Kant allowed for an indispensable use of the principle of sufficient reason, in the form that when the "conditioned" is given then so is the "unconditioned" (CPR A307-8/B364-5). In the sphere of moral philosophy, this means that the "unconditioned," in the form of the complete consequences rather than cause of morality, can be given as an ideal, which we must at least be able to believe it is possible to realize. The complete consequences of morality will turn out to include happiness, by a route that we must examine, and so the application of the principle of sufficient reason by the practical use of reason leads to the idea of "the **highest good** possible in the world" as "universal happiness combined with and in conformity with the purest morality throughout the world" (TP 8: 279). Kant's reasoning toward this conclusion will be the subject of the present section.

The background for Kant's conception of reason as always seeking a truly sufficient reason in the form of the unconditioned for anything conditioned is Kant's conception of the "logical use of reason" as the faculty of inference (CPR A303/B359). Kant envisions a syllogism as the inference of something conditioned from its condition, then pictures reason as iterating inferences from something that is conditioned to their conditions: Having found a ground for something conditioned that is itself also conditioned, reason naturally seeks the ground for that; finding this, too, to be conditioned, it again seeks a ground for this; and so on. Kant assumes that this would be an infinite regress unless it finally arrived at something that is a condition but has no condition of its own, i.e., is unconditioned. In this way the "logical maxim" – "to find the unconditioned for given cognitions of the understanding" – becomes "a principle of **pure reason** . . . that when the conditioned is given, then so is the whole series of conditions . . . which is itself unconditioned, also given," or else something unconditioned that is the condition of the whole series is given. This is something of which the mere "understanding knows nothing, since it has to do only with objects of a possible experience, whose cognition and synthesis are always conditioned" (CPR A307-8/B364-5). This thought is the origin of the three main ideas of reason and of the division of the Transcendental Dialectic of the *Critique of Pure Reason* into three main parts, the Paralogisms of Pure Reason, the Antinomy of Pure Reason, and the Ideal of Pure Reason: Kant argues that through this route reason reaches the unconditioned ideas of the spontaneous and immortal soul, the complete world-whole, and God as the necessary ground of all possibility. Since, as the Dialectic shows, these ideas outstrip the boundaries of sensibility and therefore the possibility of theoretical cognition, they can have only regulative use in guiding the conduct of theoretical inquiry. But, Kant holds, the idea of the unconditioned in general as well as these three unconditioned ideas of reason have a central role in morality: The idea of the unconditioned in general is crucial to his derivation of the idea of highest good as the object of morality, and the three ideas of reason that cannot provide theoretical knowledge become the three postulates of pure *practical* reason. Kant's complex argument begins with the idea of a complete and in that sense unconditioned *object* of morality and then turns back to the idea of the unconditioned *ground*, namely God, as the condition of the possibility of that object. Kant sometimes refers to the latter, the unconditioned ground, as the "highest original good" and the former, the unconditioned object, as the "highest derived good" (CPR A810-11/B838-9, and CPrR 5: 125).[58] As we will now see,

[58] Kant uses the same pattern in explaining the permissible regulative use of the idea of the unconditioned in theoretical philosophy: we have to postulate the existence of a completed and in that sense unconditioned system of natural laws, and then posit the existence of its unconditioned ground, a divine intelligence. See CJ, Introduction, section V, 5: 183–4.

Kant complicates things even more by introducing two different conceptions of the highest good.

The idea of the highest good was obviously of tremendous importance to Kant, not an afterthought to his moral theory: The exposition of this idea and of the practical arguments for the existence of God and the immortality of the human soul occupy the culminating position in each of the three *Critiques* and introductory positions in the two important works of 1793, the essay on "Theory and Practice" and the *Religion within the Boundaries of Mere Reason* – although any actual argument for the postulate of immortality largely disappears in the 1790s, that is, from the *Critique of the Power of Judgment* and the two works of 1793.[59] There are many differences among Kant's five treatments of the highest good,[60] but for present purposes, it will suffice to distinguish two approaches to the idea, which Kant intertwines in the first two *Critiques* but one of which he ultimately seems to favor in the works of the 1790s. Both apply the idea of the unconditioned within morality, but in different ways. The *Critique of Practical Reason* emphasizes the general role of the idea of the unconditioned in any derivation of the idea of the highest good as the ultimate object of morality: "As pure practical reason … seeks the unconditioned for the practically conditioned (which rests on inclinations and natural needs), not indeed as the determining ground of the will, but even when this is given (in the moral law), it seeks the unconditioned totality of the object of pure practical reason, under the name of the *highest good*" (CPrR, 5: 108). Kant then follows this initial statement with what we may call a conception of the *individual* highest good, based on the claim that for a person "to need happiness, to be also worthy of it, and yet not to participate it cannot be consistent with" an "impartial reason" (5: 110), although he does not say what the principle of such an impartial reason is. Here Kant is thinking of the highest good as unconditioned insofar as individual happiness completes individual moral worth, but he is also thinking of individual happiness as a conditional value constrained by the unconditioned value of motivation by respect for the moral law. Indeed, Kant has described the value of a purely moral will, committed to the moral law without reservation or restriction, as "unconditional" from the beginning of his mature work in moral philosophy (G 4: 394). He now appeals back to that opening claim in saying that "**virtue** (as worthiness to be happy) is the **supreme condition** of whatever can even seem to us desirable and hence of all our pursuit of happiness," and in that sense a "condition which is itself unconditioned, that is, not subordinate to any other" (CPrR 5: 110). But he applies the idea of the unconditioned in

[59] See Guyer 2016b.
[60] For my more detailed treatment of the highest good, see Guyer 1997 and 2011.

a second way in stating that virtue or worthiness to be happy does not thereby constitute the *complete* good for any being like a human being; "for this, **happiness** is also required." Thus Kant's conception of the highest good here seems to be a composite, in which the individual's natural end of happiness – which on Kant's account is always going to be a conception of her *own* happiness, even if that might include the happiness of *some* other people contingently close to her, such as her children or friends – is combined with, although also constrained by an antecedent commitment to morality. This can be called an individualistic conception of the highest good.

In the *Critique of Pure Reason*, however, Kant had actually begun with what may be considered a communalistic or universalistic conception of the highest good, but had then introduced the individualistic conception only as a sort of fall-back position. Kant introduces his conception of the highest good in the first *Critique* somewhat indirectly. First he defines "the world as it would be if it were in conformity with all moral laws (as it **can** be in accordance with the **freedom** of rational beings and **should** be in accordance with the necessary laws of **morality**)" as "a **moral world**" (A808/B836). Then he states the following:

> Now in an intelligible world, i.e., in the moral world, in the concept of which we have abstracted from all hindrances to morality (of the inclinations), . . . a system of happiness proportionally combined with morality can also be thought as necessary, since freedom, partly moved and partly restricted by moral laws, would itself be the cause of the general happiness, and rational beings, under the guidance of such principle, would themselves be the authors of their own enduring welfare and at the same time that of others. (A809/B838).

We can understand why freedom in accordance with moral laws should be a *restriction* on the unbridled pursuit of the natural end of one's own happiness – self-love – for Kant so frequently defines it in precisely these terms; but what can it mean that freedom "partly moved" by moral laws would itself be the *cause* of the general (in that sense complete) happiness? After all, Kant repeatedly denies that happiness is the immediate object of the moral law (G 4: 415–16; CPrR 5: 22–6, 34–6). The answer to this question is obvious if one thinks about the Formula of Humanity: If humanity is simply the capacity of human beings to set themselves ends, *and happiness is nothing but what results from the satisfaction of ends* (G 4: 418; CPrR 5: 25), then the moral command to preserve and promote the capacity to set ends is in fact equivalent to a moral command to promote happiness, and the requirement to do so to the maximal extent possible for each person compatible with doing so equally for all, expressed in the Formula of the Realm of Ends, is equivalent to a moral command to promote the happiness of all to the greatest extent compatible with equal freedom for all – what morality commands in the first instance, but not, as it turns out, all that it commands. Humanity, not happiness, is the unconditional "ground" (G 4: 428) of the fundamental principle of morality, but since humanity consists in the ability to set ends and happiness is simply the realization of ends, the complete "object" of morality is the greatest happiness of all compatible with the unconditional requirement of treating the humanity of each as an end in itself and never merely as a means – the highest good. This conception of the highest good too applies the concept of the unconditioned in two ways, in the unconditional value of the moral will and in the completed object of the moral will.

The same result can also be reached from the Formula of Universal Law, as Kant does in the Doctrine of Virtue of the *Metaphysics of Morals* when he explains why the happiness of others is an end that is also a duty. Kant's argument there, which we touched upon in the previous section, is essentially that anyone naturally wills her own happiness, which, given the analytical principle of practical reason that to will an end is to will adequate means to it, includes the maxim to will that others help her to whatever extent necessary and possible to realize her ends when her own means are insufficient. But such a maxim can only be willed *morally* if one is willing to universalize it (which, as we have seen, one could avoid only on pain of contradicting the inescapable fact that others have precisely the same kind of will one has oneself) – thus, to morally will that others (any others, as many as necessary) help one when one needs their help, one has to will to help others when they need one's help. In Kant's words, "since our self-love cannot be separated from our need to be loved (helped in case of need) by others as well, we therefore make ourselves an end for others; and the only way this maxim can be binding is through its qualification as universal law, hence through our will to make others our ends as well" (MM-DV, Introduction, section VIII.2, 6: 393). Kant does not use the phrase "highest good" in this passage, but he does explain why the happiness of others is an object or end commanded by morality itself. In his restatement of the argument in the body of the Doctrine of Virtue, he still does not use the phrase "highest good" but he makes even clearer that the happiness *of all* is the object that morality commands to be pursued *by all*:

> [E]very morally practical relation to human beings is a relation among them represented by pure reason, that is, a relation of free actions in accordance with maxims that qualify for a giving of universal law and so cannot be selfish . . . I want everyone else to be benevolent toward me . . .; hence I ought also to be benevolent toward everyone else. But since all **others** with the exception of myself would not be **all**, so that the maxim would not have

> within it the universality of a law, which is still necessary for imposing obligation, the law making benevolence a duty will include myself, as an object of benevolence, in the command of practical reason. (MM-DV, §27, 6: 450–1)

Morality is an unconditional condition in the sense of a restriction on the individual pursuit of happiness; but it also unconditionally commands the happiness of all without any restriction except that the happiness of each is commanded only as part of something complete, the happiness of all, though always subject to the restriction of equal freedom for all. The unconditional command of morality is not completed by something external to it, but itself commands happiness that is complete or unconditioned in the sense of including all. This is why "pure practical reason . . . seeks the unconditioned totality of the object of pure practical reason, under the name of the **highest good**" (CPrR 5: 108). This argument naturally leads to the universalistic conception of the highest good, namely, that the greatest morality throughout the world – each person doing his or her own moral best – would, other things being equal, lead to the greatest happiness throughout the world.

Of course, as Kant's passage on the "moral world" in the *Critique of Pure Reason* already made clear, the happiness of all, or at least the greatest happiness possible as a result of *human* actions, would follow only if *everybody* played their part, that is, "that **everyone** do what he should" (A810/B838). Bitter experience proves that all too often this condition is not satisfied. In particular, the immorality of others can thwart the happiness *of those who are moral*, for even if the morality of the latter depends on no one except themselves, their happiness, in the ordinary course of nature, can certainly depend upon the cooperation of others and be thwarted by their noncooperation. Here is where Kant seems to fall back from the collective conception of the highest good initially stated in the first *Critique* and tacitly argued for in the Doctrine of Virtue: Kant argues that the morally worthy agent surrounded by the morally unworthy must be able to hope that at least *her own* worthiness to be happy will be rewarded with happiness if her "resolve and effort" (*Vorsatz und Ausübung*, A813/B841) to be moral are not to be weakened, and this requires appeal to a power greater than her own. One's own obligation to be moral is unremitting and remains even if others are not moral, but one's hope of at least being happy oneself if one is moral also remains. Since one cannot under these circumstances hope that others will contribute to one's own happiness, one turns to God, a "**highest reason**, which commands in accordance with moral laws, as at the same time the cause of nature" (A810/B838). The morally worthy individual must be able to hope at least for her own happiness from God if not from other human beings, thus the "highest derived good" of her own happiness must depend on the "highest **original** good," God. And since there is no evidence that God delivers this happiness in "the sensible world" of ordinary nature within which our natural life spans transpire, we must assume that this reward of individual happiness for the morally worthy is bestowed in a "world that is future for us": "Thus God and a future life are two presuppositions that are not to be separated from the obligation that pure reason imposes on us in accordance with principles of that very same reason" (A811/B839) – the conditions of the possibility of the highest good are in turn these unconditioned objects, the reality of which we can now affirm on practical although not theoretical grounds.

Kant refines this picture in one way in the *Critique of Practical Reason*, although in a way that also brings out an underlying tension in his conception of the postulated God. The revision is that in the second *Critique* he describes personal immortality, "the presupposition of the **existence** and personality of the same rational being continuing **endlessly**," as postulated in order to give time enough for the perfection of individual morality, or at least for "an **endless progress** toward that complete conformity" of the individual will with the moral law that constitutes worthiness to be happy (CPrR 5: 122). The tension, however, is that he is here even more emphatic that God is postulated as the author or "supreme cause" *of a nature* "having a causality in keeping with the moral disposition" (5: 125), which presumably means that morality, including individual morality, can be efficacious *within nature*, not merely in a "life that is future for us." To put the problem bluntly, this would seem to entail that the virtuous can be promised happiness before they have perfected their virtue. This might be a motive to the endless perfection of virtue, but risks turning happiness into a premature reward.

As already mentioned, the postulate of personal immortality is deemphasized in Kant's works beginning in 1790. This goes hand in hand with an increased emphasis on the collective rather than individualistic conception of the highest good in these works. This in turn allows Kant to present the postulate of God's authorship of nature as a straightforward application of the principle that one can only rationally will that for which one believes one has potentially adequate means – which, as we saw, Kant takes to be a direct consequence of the application of the principle of noncontradiction to the concept of willing itself.

In the *Critique of the Power of Judgment*, Kant restates his moral theology in the doctrine of Method of the Critique of the Power of Teleological Judgment, his assumption being that we ultimately apply the idea of purposiveness to nature in order to perceive nature as a realm in which we can carry out our own moral objectives.[61] This restatement also turns on the idea of the unconditioned. It begins with the supposition that it is natural for us to conceive of nature as a purposive creation, and further to assume there must be something of unconditional value to be the point of this creation. Our only candidate for unconditional value is the development of our own morality. The conception of the human being as an end in itself leaves no room for a further explanation of the value of such a being: "Now of the human being (and thus of every rational being in the world), as a moral being, it cannot be further asked why (*quem in finem*) it exists. His existence contains the highest end itself, to which, as far as he is capable, he can subject the whole of nature, or against which at least he need not hold himself to be subjected to any influence from nature" (CJ, §84, 5: 435). But, Kant continues, the moral law itself sets the highest good as our moral objective: "The moral law, as the formal rational condition of the use of our freedom, obligates us by itself alone, without depending on any sort of end as a material condition," that is, without deriving its own force from any natural interest in happiness; "yet it also determines for us, and indeed does so *a priori*, a final end, to strive after which it makes obligatory for us, and this is the **highest good in the world** possible through freedom." This is "**happiness** – under the objective condition of the concordance of humans with the law of **morality**, as the worthiness to be happy" (CJ, §87, 5: 450). If morality determines *a priori* that it is obligatory for us pursue virtue or the worthiness to be happy, but also, equally *a priori*, that it is obligatory for us to pursue happiness, then this can only be the happiness of all, not just of one's own self. Further, if this happiness is to be part of the highest good possible *in the world*, this must be the natural happiness of human beings, to be achieved in the natural life span of the human species, not in some supernatural afterlife of individuals. Finally, Kant says that although it may seem "impossible for us to represent these two requirements of the final end that is set for us by the moral law" – the worthiness to be happy (of all) and happiness (of all) – "as both **connected** by merely natural causes and adequate to the idea of the final end as so conceived," nevertheless we must be able to assume that they *can be* connected. "Consequently we must assume a moral cause of the world (an author of the world) in order to set before ourselves a final end, in accordance with the moral law" (CJ, §87, 5: 451). What Kant is assuming in this final step of his argument is that while we must set the highest good possible in the world as our moral object, again, we can only will that for which we can believe we have adequate means, so we must assume that nature has an author who makes it possible for our efforts toward the

[61] I have presented the following interpretation of the culminating argument of the *Critique of the Power of Judgment* in more detail in Guyer 2001 and Guyer 2014, pp. 402–13.

highest good to be efficacious in spite of our initial impression of the inadequacy of our own powers to bring it about. Kant is now postulating God not as an author of the happiness of virtuous individuals in a life that is future for them but as the author of a nature in which human beings can, after all, and eventually, themselves bring about the highest good.

Finally, Kant's 1793 essay "On the Common Saying: That May Be Correct in Theory But It Is of No Use in Practice" takes the universal character of the highest good for granted. In a dispute with Christian Garve – who had objected that Kant's introduction of the highest good into his moral philosophy undermines it by introducing an impure motivation, namely the hope for happiness as a motivation to be virtuous – Kant had conceded that the human being is not required by morality "to **renounce** his natural end, happiness, when it is a matter of complying with his duty; for that he cannot do" – but he then argued that the concept of duty "**introduces** another end for the human being's will, namely to work to the best of one's ability toward the **highest good** possible in the world (universal happiness combined with and in conformity with the purest morality throughout the world)." Here Kant rejects the idea that hope for *one's own* eventual happiness is a condition of maintaining "support and stability" (here *Halt und Festigkeit*, words similar but not identical to those he had used in the first *Critique*); rather, Kant holds that "only in that ideal of pure reason does" the concept of duty "also get an **object**" (TP 8: 278–9). His argument again depends on the assumption that it can only be rational to strive to realize an object if one can believe adequate means for that realization are available, so we must believe in a "moral ruler of the world."[62]

Thus Kant has applied the idea of the unconditional and the principle of sufficient reason in multiple ways in his derivation of the ideal of the highest good as the necessary object of morality and of the postulation of its necessary conditions. He has applied the idea of morality as an unconditional condition on the pursuit of individual happiness, but also developed the idea of universal happiness as the complete and unconditioned object of morality itself. With reference to the former conception of the highest good he postulated personal immortality as the necessary condition of its realization, but without emphasis on either personal happiness or personal immortality he postulated the existence of God as the necessary condition of the realizability of the highest good as including universal happiness. Whatever Kant's best account of the details, he clearly thought that his concepts of the highest good and of the postulates of pure practical reason are essential parts of the rationality of morality.

[62] Here Kant does add "and in a future life," but this does seem ritualistic, since he is talking about the universal happiness that must be possible *in the world*, apparently meaning by this the world of nature and not any other.

5 Rationality and the System of Duties

In addition to the law of noncontradiction and the principle of sufficient reason, Kant's conception of reason includes the ideal of *systematicity*, although he may have conceived of this as a condition for the application of the principle of sufficient reason: The complete reason for any particular principle can only be found in its derivation from the fundamental principle of the system of which it is a part and the complete determination of its relation to all the other principles comprising that system. In the *Critique of Pure Reason*, Kant introduces the regulative ideal of systematicity in scientific knowledge as the proper contribution of pure reason to theoretical cognition after he has rejected its claim to provide speculative cognition through the unconditioned ideas of soul, world, and God. He states the teleological assumption of his entire philosophy as follows:

> Everything grounded in the nature of our powers must be purposive and consistent with their correct use, if only we can guard against a certain misunderstanding and find out their proper function. Thus the transcendental ideas too will presumably have a good and consequently **immanent** use, even though, if their significance is misunderstood and they are taken for concepts of real things, they can be transcendent in their application and for that very reason deceptive. (A642-3/B670-1)

This suggests that the ideas of the soul, the world, and God as unconditioned must have an immanent rather than a transcendent use, but Kant's first step is to analyze the immanent use of the idea of a *system* of concepts as complete and in that sense unconditioned:

> [T]he transcendental ideas are never of constitutive use, so that the concepts of certain objects would thereby be given, and in case one so understands them, they are of merely sophistical use. On the contrary, however, they have an excellent and indispensably necessary regulative use, namely that of directing the understanding to a certain goal respecting which the lines of direction of all its rules converge at one point, which, although it is only an idea ... nonetheless still serves to obtain for these concepts the greatest unity alongside the greatest extension ... what reason quite uniquely prescribes and seeks to bring about ... is the **systematic** in cognition, i.e., its interconnection based on one principle. This unity of reason always presupposes an idea, namely that of the form of a whole of cognition, which precedes the determinate cognition of the parts and contains the conditions for determining *a priori* the place of each part and its relation to the others. Accordingly, this idea postulates complete unity of the understanding's cognition, through which this cognition comes to be not merely a contingent aggregate but a system interconnected in accordance with necessary laws. (A643-5/B671-3)

Kant initially deploys this idea of systematicity in connection with *theoretical* cognition. He defines a system of scientific concepts as marked by the criteria of homogeneity, or the "systematic unity of all possible empirical concepts ... insofar as they can be derived from higher and more general ones," ultimately *one* highest principle (A652/B680); specificity, or "the demand to seek under every species that comes before us for subspecies, and for every variety smaller varieties" (A656/B684); and continuity of forms, which "arises by uniting the first two ... for then all manifolds are akin to one another, because they are all collectively descended, through every degree of extended determination, from a single highest genus" (A658/B686). Kant's predominant idea in the *Critique of Pure Reason* seems to be that the understanding can form and apply particular empirical concepts on its own, but that reason's idea of systematicity is an additional ideal of the orderliness and completeness of our empirical concepts. In the *Critique of the Power of Judgment*, however, Kant reassigns reason's ideal of systematicity to the newly introduced faculty of reflecting judgment, presumably because he now holds that the systematic organization of our knowledge is not just a nice addition to its truth but a necessary condition of our knowledge of empirical truth – a point that Kant had hinted at but not developed in the first *Critique* (A651/B679), but which he develops more fully in the Introduction(s) to the third (see especially CJ, Introduction, sections IV–V, 5: 179–86).[63]

However, Kant also treats systematicity as a necessary ideal of reason in the *practical* sphere, and here it remains a goal of reason. We may think of this form of reason as informing Kant's moral philosophy in two main ways. First, Kant supposes that we must be able to go from the single fundamental principle of morality itself to a complete and systematic array of all our particular duties – or at least of all the basic classes of our duties, since to specify all the possible circumstances of human actions and what maxims we should adopt for all those particular circumstances would be an endless task, thus the complete specification of all human duties remains just as much of an unachievable ideal as does the complete specification of all the varieties of nature in our system of empirical concepts.[64] Second, particularly in the third *Critique*, Kant restates his conception of the necessary harmony between morality and nature introduced by his concept of the highest good in terms of a single *system* of nature and freedom.

---

[63] For further discussion of these claims, see Guyer 2005, chapters 1–3.

[64] The argument of Piper 1997 that reason uses the ideal of systematicity for "hypothesis formation" in both theoretical and practical concepts is similar to this point, although I am going to bring Kant's idea of a system of duties to bear specifically on the issue of potential conflicts of duty.

Reason's requirement of systematicity in the practical as well as in the theoretical domain manifests itself in at least three ways in Kant's suggestions about the derivation of duties from the fundamental principle of morality. First, in his initial version of what he identifies as a third formulation of the categorical imperative, Kant suggests that the test of eligibility as universal law is to be applied not just to individual proposed maxims considered in isolation, but to the whole body of our (that is, any agent's and all agents') proposed maxims:

> the **principle** of every human will as **a will giving universal law through all its maxims** . . . would be very **well suited** to be the categorical imperative . . . if there is a categorical imperative (i.e., a law for every will of a rational being) it can only command that everything be done from the maxim of one's will as a will that could at the same time have as its object itself as giving universal law. (G 4: 432)

The requirements that *all* of anyone's maxims pass the test of universalizability, or that "everything be done" in accordance with this principle, and that this is a law for the will of *every* rational being, imply that moral maxims must form an intra- and interpersonal system. Although Kant does not use the term "system" here, what reason here requires is precisely what he defines as "the **systematic** in cognition, i.e., its interconnection based on one principle" (CPR A645/B673).

In his second version of the third formulation of the categorical imperative, Kant does use the term "system" explicitly. This is the Formula of the Realm of Ends, which Kant derives from the previous formulation that every rational being must regard himself as giving universal law through all the maxims of his will. Here Kant says:

> Now since laws determine ends in terms of their universal validity, if we abstract from the personal differences of rational beings as well as from all content of their private ends we shall be able to think of a whole of all ends in systematic connection (a whole both of rational beings as ends in themselves and of the ends of his own that each may set himself), that is, a realm of ends, which is possible in accordance with the above principles. (G 4: 433)

As Kant says a few pages later, this formulation of the categorical imperative represents a "complete determination of all maxims" because all maxims have both form and matter. The form is universality, and the matter is always an end. In the first instance, what Kant has in mind is rational beings as ends in themselves – "in this respect the formula says that a rational being, as an end by its nature and hence as an end in itself, must in every maxim serve as the limiting condition of all merely relative and arbitrary ends" (G 4: 436) – and so what reason requires of us, through the categorical imperative, is that we act so that all persons, not just some, are treated as ends in themselves. This yields a systematic union of persons in which each is indeed treated as an end. But the humanity of persons, which makes them ends in themselves, consists in their ability to set *particular* ends for themselves freely; so in requiring of each and every person that they treat the humanity in themselves and all others as a system of ends, reason is also requiring of all persons that they select only particular ends for themselves that are compatible with the free choice of such ends by all others as well, in other words are compatible with a "systematic connection . . . of the ends of his own that each may set himself."

Third, Kant's derivation of particular duties always takes the form of a system, an exhaustive division based on a single principle in which each duty has its proper place. He describes such a system schematically in the *Groundwork*, when, as we saw, he argues for the adequacy of his first and second formulations of the categorical imperative by showing that they both give rise to the commonly accepted exhaustive division of duties into perfect and imperfect duties to self and others (G 4: 421n). Kant explicitly refers to his presentation of ethical duties in the Doctrine of Virtue of the *Metaphysics of Morals* as a system:

> [W]e shall set forth the system in two parts: the **doctrine** of the **elements of ethics** and the **doctrine** of the **methods of ethics**. Each part will have its divisions. In the first part, these will be made in accordance with the different **subjects** to whom human beings are under obligation; in the second part, in accordance with the different **ends** that reason puts them under obligation to have, and with their receptivity to these ends. (MM-DV, Introduction, section XVII, 6: 412).

Kant says that ethics in particular "unavoidably leads to questions that call upon judgment to decide how a maxim is to be applied . . . because of the latitude it allows in its imperfect duties" (6: 411). But in fact the whole of the *Metaphysics of Morals* describes a system of duties (as Kant promised in the *Groundwork* that it would eventually do) when it divides duties into the logically exhaustive classes of duties of right and virtue, that is, the coercively enforceable and the noncoercively enforceable duties; the coercively enforceable duties of right, which are all duties to others, into those concerning innate right and acquired right; the noncoercively enforceable duties into those to self and those to others; and the latter finally into duties of love and duties of respect. All of these duties are supposed to be derivable from a single principle,[65] and although in both

[65] Thomas Pogge, Marcus Willaschek, and Allen Wood have argued that the foundational principle of Kant's system of duties of right, the Universal Principle of Justice, is *not* derived from or an application of the fundamental principle of morality. I argue against this claim in Guyer 2002 and 2016c (which provide references), and here add that although Kant holds that duties of right *may* be satisfied because of fear of sanctions ("aversive external incentives"), he also holds that they

parts of the *Metaphysics of Morals* Kant alludes both to the requirement of the universalizability of maxims and to the principle that humanity must always be treated as an end in itself, he has made it clear in the *Groundwork* that he regards these as interchangeable, or at least as coextensive, thus as at bottom a single principle. And when what follows from a single underlying principle is divided into an exhaustive scheme of genera and species – in this case of duties – we have a system as demanded by reason.

Why might we need a *system* of duties? To be sure that we have correctly formulated the fundamental principle of morality and recognized all our main kinds of duty as following from it? Yes, but for another reason as well. In the introduction to the *Metaphysics of Morals* Kant remarks that there can be no *conflicts* of duties, only conflicts of "grounds of obligation," potential reasons for duties or, as a later tradition would say, *prima facie* or *pro tanto* duties but not duties all things considered.[66] Kant supposes that any time there is a conflict between grounds of obligation there is a correct resolution of that conflict in favor of one ground or the other, which then becomes the actual duty to be fulfilled in the circumstances at hand: "A **conflict of duties** (*collisio officiorum s. obligationum*) would be a relation between them in which one of them would cancel the other (wholly or in part). – But since duty and obligation are concepts that express the objective practical necessity of certain actions and two rules opposed to each other cannot be necessary at the same time" – *this is clearly an application of reason's fundamental law of noncontradiction* – "if it is a duty to act in accordance with one rule, to act in accordance with the opposite rule is not a duty but even contrary to duty; so a **collision of duties** and obligations is inconceivable (*obligationes non colliduntur*) " (MM Introduction, section III, 6: 224). Here is where Kant might have brought in the principle of excluded middle as well as that of noncontradiction: whereas the latter principle tells us that two contrary duties, that is, duties to perform two incompatible acts at the same time, cannot both be duties (on the ground that we cannot have an obligation to perform the impossible), the former would tell us that we have to perform one of these duties. But *which* one? Kant does not say much about *how* potential conflicts among grounds of obligation are to be resolved except to state that "[w]hen two such grounds conflict with each other, practical philosophy says, not that the stronger obligation takes precedence (*fortior obligatio*

can be fulfilled from respect for the moral law, which could not be the case unless fulfillment of these duties were *required* by the moral law. Wood's most recent defense of the "independence" thesis tacitly concedes that it comes to nothing more than that duties of right do not require compliance out of respect for the idea of duty itself; see Wood 2014, ch. 3, pp. 70–89, especially p. 83.

[66] This is the tradition of early twentieth-century British "intuitionism," identified especially with Sir David Ross; see Ross 1930.

vincit) but that the stronger **ground of obligation** prevails (*fortior obligandi ratio vincit*)." But what makes one ground of obligation stronger than another?

Georg Friedrich Meier, who wrote not only the logic text that Kant used but lengthy textbooks in moral philosophy as well, had explicitly argued that a systematic classification of duties has the potential to eliminate what might otherwise be conflicts of duties by hierarchically or lexically ordering them. "No true duty," Meier asserted, "and no true moral rule, can contradict another true duty, and another true moral rule." Sometimes, Meier argued, apparent conflicts can easily be resolved simply by attending to the different duties at different times, but sometimes the resolution of apparent conflicts requires a lexical ordering of duties: "In the general theory of the practical disciplines it is demonstrated that we are obligated by a duty only so far as it is possible" (in other words, ought implies can, and the contrapositive as well); "consequently also only in those cases in which it can be observed without detriment to all other higher duties."[67] Meier then uses the word "systematic" in his description of the moral life as the satisfaction of a coherent set of duties:

> The greatest perfection of practical philosophy [is] that therein the natural duties are connected to one another in the best and most excellent order . . . For the sake of the whole end of these disciplines it is not sufficient that one be convinced that an action is a duty; one must also know whether a duty is a higher or lower duty, a more important and necessary one or [less] indispensable and necessary; whether it is a chief duty or an ancillary one; whether it must be fulfilled prior to another or subsequent to it? Our entire moral life must be an orderly observation of all our duties. What we must do first we must not postpone, and what we must do foremost we must not do only by-the-by. The virtuous life must not be a disorderly and tumultuous observation of our duties, but a systematic and methodical observation of the laws.[68]

This paragraph is already longer than what Kant has to say about the resolution of apparent conflicts of duties, and then the five fat volumes of Meier's *Philosophical Doctrine of Morals* lay out the complete system of duties in which potential conflicts of duties can be resolved by showing which ground of obligation is higher, which lower, which must be satisfied first and which only later, and so on – volumes I and II lay out our duties to God, which Kant explicitly drops from his own system (e.g., MM-DV, §18, 6: 443–4); volumes II and III our duties to ourselves; volume IV our duties toward other people; and volume V duties arising from special positions, such as that of the scholar.[69] Kant does not explicitly state that we need a system of duties to resolve potential conflicts of duties, but perhaps he does not need to because Meier had so

[67] Meier 1764, §8, p. 21. [68] Meier 1764, §19, pp. 42–3. [69] Meier 1762–74.

explicitly asserted the point. Kant's system of duties has the same form as Meier's, so it may be assumed that Kant intended his system of duties to play the same role as Meier's, that of telling us how to live a life in which we satisfy our obligations in an orderly and coherent fashion, resolving potential conflicts of duty in a rational manner.

Kant does not explicitly state that his system of duties yields a *hierarchy* of duties. Perhaps he assumes that the basic distinction between perfect and imperfect duties does much of the necessary work: perfect duties seem to admit of no exceptions, therefore they need to be satisfied before you can fulfill imperfect duties, although they can often be satisfied just by omissions of proscribed types of actions – for example, you cannot murder, rob, or defraud in order to get money to pay for your own education, even if that would count as self-improvement or self-perfection. You cannot use money you need to pay back a voluntarily incurred debt to help others, no matter how genuinely needy they may be; only once your debts have been satisfied can you consider being charitable. But the precedence of perfect over imperfect duties hardly resolves all potential conflicts among grounds of obligation. Conflicts between perfect duties at least seem possible, and conflicts between imperfect duties are certainly possible, as when I feel a conflict between some possible act of self-perfection and some possible act of beneficence toward others. Since the imperfect duties are only duties to (sincerely) adopt certain ends, not to perform specific types of actions on every possible occasion, perhaps the latter type of conflict can be resolved by one of the considerations Meier suggests – temporal sequencing – and perhaps by consequentialist considerations as well – maybe I should study for my medical exams rather than working at the soup kitchen today because that way I will be in a position to help more people in the future than I could help now. As long as consequentialist considerations have not entered into the fundamental principle of morality or one's motivation for acting in accordance with it, it is not obvious that such considerations cannot enter into its application: Indeed, since the duty of beneficence is imperfect, it seems only natural to remedy its indeterminacy by deciding in a particular case for an action that will help more people rather than fewer. Perhaps lexical ordering is possible within the domain of perfect duties as well – maybe the duty not to take the life of oneself or another rightly takes precedence over preserving the possibility of some particular instance of free agency by oneself or another, such as telling the truth on some particular occasion, for such freedom could be restored on future occasions in a way that life itself cannot. Kant does not explicitly assert such hierarchical relationships among perfect duties. Perhaps perfect duties do not always even trump imperfect duties – for example, perhaps the imperfect duty to render assistance, such as to try to help a person in mortal danger, should override the duty to keep a relatively unimportant promise, such as one to meet a friend for lunch (assuming that the duty to *keep* promises, as opposed to the duty not to make false promises that you do not *intend* to keep, is a perfect duty in the first place – which it is probably not, since keeping a promise is not always in your own power). But although Kant hardly worked out all the details, the organization of the *Metaphysics of Morals*, which expounds first perfect duties to self and others (some of the latter of which are coercibly enforceable as duties of right), then imperfect duties to self, and only then imperfect duties to others, can at least be read as if it presents a hierarchy of duties for the resolution of potential conflicts among them.[70]

Kant's second main application of the idea of systematicity as a demand of reason in his moral philosophy is the idea, as he puts it in the third *Critique*, that the two legislations of the theoretical and the practical uses of reason must be joined together into a single coherent view. This is a way of restating the thesis of the first *Critique* that the natural world must be able to be transformed into a moral world (A809/B837) and the argument of the second *Critique* that the possibility of realizing the highest good requires the postulation of a "supreme cause of nature having a causality in keeping with the moral disposition" (5: 125). But when Kant presents as the defining issue for the third *Critique* demonstrating that the "concept of freedom" should and therefore *can* have an influence on the "domain of the concept of nature" – "namely the concept of freedom should make the end that is imposed by its laws real in the sensible world; and nature must consequently also be able to be conceived in such a way that the lawfulness of its form is at least in agreement with the possibility of the ends that are to be realized in it in accordance with the laws of freedom" (CJ, Introduction, Section II, 5: 176) – he explicitly puts the issue as one of systematicity. We have already considered this argument; here I will merely add that Kant explicitly characterizes the chief argument of the Critique of Teleological Judgment, namely that our experience of organisms leads us to think of them as purposive, an attitude that we then inevitably extend to the whole of nature precisely because of the unity of our reason, and can then redeem only by seeing the whole of nature as a means to the realization of the unconditional moral goal of human beings – freedom – in terms of the concept of a system:

> It is therefore only matter insofar as it is organized that necessarily carries with it the concept of itself as a natural end, since its specific form is at the same time a product of nature. However, this concept necessarily leads to the idea of the whole of nature as a system in accordance with the rule of ends, to

[70] I have developed this suggestion in Guyer 2005, pp. 243–74, and Guyer 2014, pp. 276–86.

> which idea all of the mechanism of nature in accordance with principles of reason must now be subordinated . . . one is justified, indeed called upon to expect nothing in nature and its laws but what is purposive in the whole. (CJ, §67, 5: 378–9)

In the culminating argument of the third *Critique* (which in a way is also the culminating argument of Kant's entire philosophy and therefore of his moral philosophy as well), what sometimes seem like two separate requirements of reason, namely that we seek the unconditioned and systematicity, clearly come together, for Kant ultimately assumes that a system must have not only a single fundamental principle but also a single final end, and that this end as well as this principle must be unconditioned. Because nothing unconditioned is ever given in nature, which is given only through sensibility, "the final end cannot be an end that nature would be sufficient to produce." The only end that can be represented as "unconditioned and independent of natural conditions but yet as necessary in itself" is the realization of human freedom, which is supersensible, but in turn sets an object for itself "as the highest end (the highest good in the world)" (CJ, §84, 5: 435). Thus, Kant supposes that, by making the unconditioned its ideal, pure reason requires that we view nature as a system that makes possible the realization of the highest good in accordance with the moral law, although, since freedom itself is supersensible, nature itself cannot be regarded as necessitating our free choice to realize that goal through a systematic choice of maxims and particular ends. That remains an act of human freedom.

6 Reason as Motivation

This completes our survey of Kant's derivation of the content of morality from the fundamental principles of reason in general. But it is also part of Kant's project in moral philosophy to show that pure reason can be *practical* in the sense that "pure reason of itself suffices to determine the will," indeed that "it alone, and not reason empirically limited," that is, instrumental reasoning in behalf of some merely empirical inclination, "is unconditionally practical" (CPrR 5: 15). Part of what is necessary in order to show that pure reason is practical is that the human will is always free to act in accordance with the demands of pure reason, in other words that we have free will, and a central argument of the *Critique of Practical Reason* is the proof that we do have free will, carried out within the framework of transcendental idealism. This is the central argument of Chapter I of the Analytic of Pure Practical Reason in the *Critique of Practical Reason*, and we touched upon it earlier. But Chapter III of the Analytic, entitled "On the Incentives of Pure Practical Reason," describes the phenomenal character of motivation by pure reason – not so much the underlying metaphysics of motivation by pure reason but what the experience of what this is like. This is what I will briefly discuss in the present section.

Kant's view that reason can motivate us may seem to be diametrically opposed to Hume's position that reason is motivationally inert and that only sentiment, not reason, can move us to action. From this Hume had inferred that moral principles themselves are grounded in sentiment, not on reason: "Morals excite passions, and produce or prevent actions. Reason of itself is utterly impotent in this particular. The rules of morality, therefore, are not conclusions of our reason."[71] Kant agrees with Hume that moral principles are "suppos'd to influence our passions and actions,"[72] but he supposes that reason *can* do this and therefore that reason can be the source of moral principles. Kant might seem to think that reason can move us to action *instead of* and independently from passions, sentiments, or feelings of any kind, as when he opens the "Incentives" chapter by stating that "What is essential to any moral worth of actions is **that the moral law determine the will immediately**" (CPrR 5: 71): "immediately" seems to mean precisely without intervention of any kind, therefore without the intervention of any kind of feeling. In the Introduction to the Doctrine of Virtue in the *Metaphysics of Morals*, however, Kant states that "Every determination of choice [*Willkür*] proceeds **from the representation of a possible action** to the deed *through the feeling of pleasure or displeasure*, taking an interest in the action or its effect" (MM-DV, Introduction, section XII.a, 6: 399, italics added). If we are to find a consistent theory of moral motivation in Kant, these two statements have to be reconciled.

They can be reconciled in the following way. On Kant's theory of transcendental idealism, freedom of the will – in its most basic form the freedom to choose whether or not to make the moral law one's most fundamental maxim, subordinating all other incentives, under the name of self-love, to it (Rel 6: 36), or the freedom to choose whether or not to make pure rather than merely empirical, instrumental reason one's fundamental principle – is an act of the *noumenal* self, the self that is not spatiotemporal and is therefore free from the grip of deterministic causality (see especially CPR A448-50/B476-8). Since feelings are clearly occurrences in space and time, specifically, as occurrences in inner sense, in time, they are no part of the noumenal world, so the noumenal choice of fundamental maxim cannot be based on feeling – this choice is, in Kant's favorite term, simply "inscrutable," inexplicable (CPrR 5: 47). However, although the noumenal act of choice for or against the moral law is supposed to

[71] Hume 1739–40, Book III, Part I, section I, paragraph 6.
[72] Hume 1739–40, Book III, Part I, section I, paragraph 5.

be "immediate," Kant's theory is that at the *phenomenal* level, that is to say, in the natural world, this choice of fundamental maxim produces action *by first producing a feeling*, namely the feeling of respect, or, in Kant's ultimate and fuller theory, by *strengthening and cultivating* an array of natural, inborn "aesthetic preconditions of the mind's susceptibility to concepts of duty," namely moral feeling, conscience, love of others or sympathy, and self-respect or self-esteem (MM-DV, Introduction, section XII, 6: 399–403). The noumenal choice of fundamental maxim may be the ultimate cause of morally worthy action, yet the phenomenal, proximate cause of such action *is feeling*, but feeling either produced or cultivated under the aegis of the agent's fundamental commitment to the moral law. This is the way in which the (noumenal) determination of choice by the moral law proceeds from the representation of a possible action to the performance of the action – or, as we will see, the adoption of particular maxims of action – through the feeling of pleasure or displeasure. Reason produces action – here is Kant's disagreement with Hume – but it does so through the production or modification of feeling – here is Kant's agreement with Hume.

Kant developed this view only gradually. In the *Groundwork*, Section I offers an analysis of the condition for moral worth, namely a good will, which to imperfectly rational beings like us human beings presents itself in the form of duty. Kant analyzes what it is to act not merely *in conformity with* duty but *from* duty as one's motive in the following form: Action from duty is not action for the sake of an inclination, it is therefore not action for the sake of any object of inclination; if neither inclination nor an object of inclination can determine the dutiful or good will, then all that is left is the form of its maxim, namely its universalizability; "hence there is left for the [good or dutiful] will nothing that could determine it except objectively the [form of] **law** and subjectively **pure respect** for this practical law, and so the maxim of complying with such a law even if it infringes upon all my inclinations" (G 4: 400–1). We can understand this statement by analogy to the relation between a proposition and a propositional attitude: The content of the good will is the moral law and the attitude of the good will toward it is affirmation, or determination to act in accordance with it. This is an abstract conception of "pure respect," with no particular phenomenology implied. In a footnote, however, Kant states that respect is a *feeling*, although "not one **received** by means of influence" from ordinary sensibility; "it is instead a feeling **self-wrought** by means of a rational concept and therefore specifically different from all feelings of the first kind, which can be reduced to inclination or fear." So Kant claims that pure reason, or the determination of the will by pure reason, can produce a distinctive feeling, one that is neither inclination nor fear "though it has something analogous to both." But in this note Kant assigns no distinctive role to this feeling in the production of action; rather he says that "[i]mmediate determination of the will by means of the law and consciousness of this is called **respect**, so this is regarded as the **effect** of the law on the subject, and not as the **cause** of the law. Respect is properly the representation of a worth that infringes upon my self-love," which is why it has something analogous to fear, although it is "nevertheless a product of our [own] will," which is why it has an analogy with inclination, that is, is pleasant as well as painful (G 4: 401n). Yet the feeling seems to be only the *consciousness* of the determination of the will by the moral law, the way this presents itself to creatures like us, and to play a role neither in the determination of the will to abide by the moral law in the first place nor in the transmission of this determination to the choice of particular maxims of action or the performance of particular actions in accordance with such maxims.

In the *Critique of Practical Reason*'s chapter on the incentives of pure practical reason, Kant moves toward a position in which the feeling of respect plays a causal role, not in the fundamental determination of the will to abide by the moral law, but in the transmission of this determination to the performance of particular actions in the phenomenal world, through the selection of particular maxims in the phenomenal world. The chapter begins, as has already been noted, with the statement, "What is essential to any moral worth of actions is **that the moral law determine the will immediately**" (CPrR 5: 71); so Kant is not conceding that the feeling of respect plays any essential role in the fundamental determination of the will to abide by the moral law – for Kant, that is an action of the noumenal will, in a domain where a phenomenal event like a feeling *could* not play a causal role. Kant then goes on to describe, more fully than in the *Groundwork* but along the same lines, how this determination of the (noumenal) will by the moral law or pure reason produces a feeling: It strikes down "self-conceit," or the disposition to make self-love one's fundamental principle, which is painful; but since the moral law that strikes down self-conceit "is still something in itself positive – namely, the form of an intellectual causality, that is of freedom . . . it is an object of the greatest **respect** and so too the ground of a positive feeling," that is, a feeling of pleasure, "that is not of empirical origin and is cognized *a priori*" (CPrR 5: 73). So far, the feeling of respect is still described only as an effect of the immediate determination of the will by the moral law, and has been ascribed no further causal role. As Kant continues, however, he does assign the feeling of respect a causal role, at least at the phenomenal level of action: He continues to maintain that the feeling is "**practically effected**" (*gewirkt*), that is, caused by the (noumenal) determination of the will by pure reason's moral law, but now adds that this "representation of the moral law deprives self-love of its influence and self-conceit of its illusion, and thereby the hindrance to pure practical reason is lessened and the representation of the superiority of its objective law to the impulses of sensibility is produced, and hence, by removal of the counterweight, the relative weightiness of the law (in regard to a will affected by impulses)" is also produced. "And so respect for the law is not the incentive to morality" but it "supplies authority to the law, which now alone has influence" (CPrR 5: 75–6). All this makes it sound as if the feeling of respect "supplies authority to the law" by counterbalancing and ultimately outweighing other inclinations or feelings at the phenomenal level, where particular actions take place. The feeling of respect "infringes upon the activity of the subject so far as inclinations are his determining grounds" (5: 78). Kant further states that respect for the law "must be regarded as a subjective ground of activity – that is, as the incentive to compliance with the law – and as the ground for maxims of a course of life in conformity with it" (5: 79). This suggests that although the feeling of respect does not play a role in the (noumenal) choice to make the moral law one's *fundamental* maxim, it does play a role in selecting *particular* maxims, in the course of a phenomenal life in conformity with the moral law as one's fundamental maxim, and that it therefore plays a role in the phenomenal production of actions by playing this role in the selection of the particular maxims by means of which they are chosen. (Indeed, the choice of particular maxims can only be imagined as taking place in the phenomenal world, because they presuppose empirical knowledge of one's spatiotemporal situation, what ends are possible, what means to those ends are causally possible in it, and so forth.) In this way the feeling of respect plays an essential role in the transmission of the (noumenal) determination of the will to actions in the (phenomenal) world.

In the *Metaphysics of Morals*, Kant suggests an even more detailed theory of how the determination of the will by pure reason leads to actions in the phenomenal world. This theory is suggested in two places, in the Introduction to the Doctrine of Virtue and in the discussion of duties of love toward others in the body of that text. Section XII of the Introduction to the Doctrine of Virtue is entitled "Aesthetic Preconditions [*Ästhetische Vorbegriffe*] of the Mind's Receptivity to Concepts of Duty in General." It is here that Kant states, as already quoted, that "[e]very determination of choice proceeds **from the representation of a possible action to** the deed through the feeling of pleasure or displeasure, taking an interest in the action or its effect" (6: 399). By "aesthetic preconditions" Kant means feelings or effect on feeling. He continues by stating that "The state of **feeling** here (the way in which inner sense is affected) is either **pathological** or **moral**. – The former is that feeling which precedes the representation of the law; the latter, that which can only follow upon it," and we can infer that in the latter case feeling gives rise to an interest in an action itself while in the former case, that of inclination, the interest is in the effect of the actions on one's own condition or that of someone else in whom an agent has a contingent interest. The crucial point, however, is that in the case of a moral effect on feeling, it is the representation of the moral law, which is given by reason itself, as well as the determination of the will to make the moral law its fundamental maxim, and no doubt further the recognition that a particular maxim of action falls under the moral law, the result of a practical syllogism performed by practical reason, which causes the feeling of pleasure or the effect upon feeling, but that feeling in turn that leads to the deed (*Tat*); in other words, moral feeling produced by reason (or as it will turn out, cultivated under the guidance of reason) is in turn the proximate cause of the action called for by moral reasoning. Whether the determination of the will by the moral law is conceived of as an act of the noumenal will, as it is by Kant, or as an act of the natural person, as it is by most others, it leads to action *through its effect on our feelings*. Here Kant unreservedly assigns moral feeling an indispensable place in the phenomenal production of action.

In Section XII of the Introduction, Kant enumerates four "aesthetic preconditions of the mind's susceptibility to concepts of duty." These are moral feeling, which makes "us aware of the constraint present in the thought of duty" (6: 399); conscience, which is "practical reason holding the human being's duty before him for his acquittal or condemnation in every case that comes under a law" (6: 400); love of human beings, or benevolence, which is a felt disposition to help others (6: 402); and respect in the sense of "self-esteem" (*Selbstschätzung*), which is a feeling that "is the basis of certain duties, that is, of certain actions that are consistent with [one's] duty to himself" (6: 403). Kant's idea seems to be that moral feeling is a general feeling of pleasure at the idea of conforming to the moral law and of displeasure at the idea of violating it; that conscience, which is not itself a feeling, is the disposition to examine whether particular cases that arise in the actual world, or maxims that are suggested, conform to the moral law or not, and the disposition to feel pleasure or displeasure in response; that love of others is a feeling specifically concerned with the idea of performing beneficent actions toward them; and that self-esteem is a feeling directed toward oneself and prompting the fulfillment of duties to oneself. About the feeling of love toward (other) human beings, Kant actually says that it is a feeling that will eventually *follow* the performance of beneficent actions toward them, so it does not seem to function as the proximate cause of beneficent actions: "If someone practices [beneficence] often and succeeds in realizing his beneficent intention, he eventually comes actually to love the person he has helped" (6: 403). About moral feeling, conscience, and self-esteem, however, what Kant says is that these are naturally occurring dispositions, without which one would be "morally dead," that is, completely unreceptive to the call of morality (6: 400), but all of which need to be cultivated and strengthened. Kant is not very clear on how this is to be done, saying only in the case of moral feeling that it is to be strengthened "through wonder at its inscrutable source." But the general point is that recognition of the moral law through reason will lead us to cultivate and strengthen conscience and the feelings that constitute our receptivity to morality, that is, the natural dispositions that actually make it possible for us to perform the deeds that morality requires at the phenomenal level of our existence. Reason does not simply lead to action *instead of feeling* doing so; reason leads to action by *affecting* our feelings, specifically by leading us to cultivate feelings (and conscience) to which we must but also do have a natural predisposition.

In his treatment of duties of love toward others in the body of the Doctrine of Virtue, Kant makes this general point clear, and revises and refines his treatment of feelings of love toward others to better fit the model of the "aesthetic preconditions" as the proximate cause of the actions called for by morality. Here Kant divides the general category of "duties of love" into the three duties of beneficence, gratitude, and sympathy (MM-DV, §29, 6: 452). This division might seem to multiply the duties that one has toward others beyond beneficence, but what Kant seems to mean is that beneficence is the positive duty of helping others who need help when it is within one's means to help them (when one has the resources to do so and doing so is consistent with all one's other duties, so as to avoid collisions of duty), and that gratitude and sympathy are feelings that can prompt one to be beneficent on specific occasions and that ought to be cultivated so that they will be adequate to doing so when that is appropriate. Thus "beneficence is the maxim of making others' happiness one's end, and the duty to it consists in the subject's being constrained by his reason to adopt this maxim as a universal law" (6: 452); beneficence itself is the primary duty of love to others enjoined directly by reason. But gratitude is a feeling of respect for a benefactor that can become an "active" rather than merely "affective" feeling (§31.B, 6: 454–5), that is, presumably, which can prompt one who feels it toward beneficent action, and which ought to be cultivated and strengthened for that reason.

Kant does not go into great detail on how gratitude leads to action, but he does say that it can lead the agent "to render **equal** services to the benefactor if he can receive them (if he is still living), or, if he cannot, to render them to others" (§33, 6: 456). That is, sometimes one will be able to perform a beneficent act toward a person who has previously been beneficent to oneself, and in that case the feeling of gratitude may not only prompt a beneficent action but so to speak target it, that is, make determinate how one can fulfill the otherwise indeterminate, imperfect duty of beneficence. In other cases, the benefactor might not need one's beneficence in return, but then the subject's gratitude might prompt him to help others in the way that he was helped, which would again both target and prompt his beneficent actions. For example, someone who benefited from an endowed scholarship might not be able to benefit his benefactor in any particular way, but once the student has himself become successful because of the education he received, he could be prompted by his gratitude toward his own benefactor to endow a similar benefaction for successive generations of needy students. Whatever the details, Kant says that gratitude "combine[s] the **cordiality** of a benevolent disposition with **sensitivity** to benevolence" and provides an opportunity "to cultivate one's love of human beings" (6: 456). Gratitude is a form of feeling that can be cultivated and, when properly cultivated, leads to and does not just follow beneficent actions.

Sympathy is the other feeling that Kant addresses under the rubric of duties of love. He conceives of sympathy as sharing another's emotional response to the situation in which the other finds herself: "**Sympathetic joy** and **sadness** (*sympathia moralis*) are sensible feelings of pleasure or displeasure (which are therefore to be called 'aesthetic') at another state of joy or pain (shared feeling, sympathetic feeling)" (MM-DV, §34, 6:456). Kant's use of the word "aesthetic" here clearly connects the present treatment of sympathy with his earlier discussion of the "aesthetic preconditions of the mind's susceptibility to concepts of duty" – sympathetic feeling is now being offered as such a condition. In fact, Kant is more concerned with sympathetic pain at another's suffering than with sympathetic pleasure at another's good fortune, since he conceives of sympathetic feeling as a prompt to help others who are in need, not as any reason to try to add something to their good fortune. Sympathy, which is to say sympathetic pain, is to be used "as a means to promoting active and rational benevolence," that is to say, beneficence – sympathetic feelings are the prompt to or proximate cause of beneficent actions, and our disposition to such feelings is to be cultivated and strengthened because they play such a role.

According to Kant, "Nature has already implanted in human beings receptivity to such feelings," but "to use this as a means of implanting active and rational benevolence is . . . a particular, though only conditional duty" (§34, 6: 456). Because nature has implanted the disposition to such feelings in us, our duty with regard to them is not to try to create them out of whole cloth, but to "cultivate the compassionate natural (aesthetic) feelings in us." This is done by not avoiding "the places where the poor who lack the most basic necessities are to be found but rather [by] seek[ing] them out, and not [shunning] sickrooms and debtors' prisons and so forth in order to avoid sharing painful feelings one may not be able to resist" (§35, 6: 457). Presumably making such visits trains us to overcome our natural aversion to sharing the painful feelings of others and thereby allows us to strengthen our own feelings in order to be able to use them to perform the beneficent acts for which such situations will often call. Kant calls the duty to strengthen such feelings or our capacity to feel them and then to act upon them "a particular, though only conditional duty" (§34, 6: 456), meaning in the first instance that this duty is "indirect," that is, that it is not a duty simply to have such feelings, which cannot be summoned out of thin air if the tendency to have them is not already present, but a duty to strengthen that tendency to feel them just because they are proximate causes of beneficent actions. Kant points out that it is not a general duty to feel the pain of others, because it is not a duty to do so in situations in which one can do nothing for those others, thus in such situations feeling their pain would only add to the pain in the world, and "there cannot possibly be a duty to increase the ills in the world" (§34, 6: 457). Our duty is to cultivate such feelings so that we will feel them with adequate strength in the situations in which they can prompt us to beneficent actions that we can perform.

There is a second sense in which our duty to cultivate sympathetic feeling is "conditional," which Kant does not make explicit but which is clearly implied by his whole model of the relation between moral reason and feeling. This is that our duty to act upon such feelings can only be a duty to act upon them in situations in which they would prompt us to perform morally appropriate actions, and thus our duty to cultivate can only be the duty to cultivate and strengthen our disposition to have and act upon such feelings in such situations. An example offered by Barbara Herman can bring this point home.[73] It is in general appropriate to act upon our feelings of sympathy toward persons struggling with difficult tasks by helping them, for example, assisting someone struggling with a heavier package than he can manage on his own. But sometimes we ought not to act even on our well-developed feelings of sympathy. For example, if we see someone struggling with a heavy package outside the back door of the art museum in the middle of the night, we ought not to act upon our immediate inclination to help; instead we should probably call the police. Herman uses this example to introduce the idea that there are "rules of moral salience" that can alert us to situations that call for moral judgment, which is itself something that has to be practiced. Kant does not speak of rules of moral salience, nor is it clear that he thinks we could formulate rules of thumb that would allow us readily sort out situations in which it would be appropriate to act

[73] See Herman 1993, ch. 1.

as our well-cultivated feelings prompt us to do so and situations in which these feelings must be resisted. Instead, Kant would appeal to conscience: While in many situations it may be obvious what morality demands, sometimes it will not be obvious, and in these cases we need to stop and reflect, that is, bring the case before the bench of the moral law and ask whether the maxim that we are prompted by our feelings to act upon is universalizable or not, or whether it treats the humanity of everyone involved (future museumgoers as well as the art thief, in our example) as an end and not merely as a means. While the general maxim to help anyone else in need when one can would pass the test of universalization, presumably the more narrowly defined maxim to help people engaged in theft would not.

Kant's treatment of sympathetic feelings thus suggests that reason, through its determination of the will by the moral law, will lead us to strengthen and cultivate the kinds of feelings that can lead to morally requisite "deeds," but will also provide a check on such laws, in the form of conscience, in cases where it would not be morally appropriate to act as they suggest. This can be taken as Kant's final position on the relation between reason and feeling in moral action. This model makes clear that it is not Kant's view that the morally worthy person must act from reason *rather* than feeling, but rather that the morally worthy person acts *from* feeling, but from feelings that have been cultivated under the guidance of reason and that are allowed to lead to action under the constraint of reason. This tells us how to read the concluding sentence of Kant's treatment of sympathy: "this is still one of the impulses that nature has implanted in us to do what the representation of duty alone might not accomplish" (§35, 6: 457). This does not mean that it would be best to act from the (rational) representation of duty alone, but that if that is not strong enough to make us do what we should then it is at least second best to act out of feelings such as sympathy. Rather, it means that in creatures like us, who are animal as well as rational, reason does not work through the representation of rules alone, but works precisely by leading us to cultivate and act upon feelings, though it also constrains our action upon feelings in accordance with moral laws when that is necessary. Feelings are not fall-backs, but, when properly cultivated and constrained, are precisely the natural means to morally worthy actions in creatures like us – the means that reason uses to achieve the goals it sets for us.

This completes my survey of how reason determines the content of morality and how it motivates us to act morally. Before concluding, however, I want to say a few words about Kant's methodology, or, in contemporary terms, his metaethics. This comment will take the form of a brief discussion of what is currently called "Kantian constructivism."

7 Kantian Constructivism

A major debate in recent metaethics has been that between moral realism and constructivism.[74] Many interpretations of Kant and moral philosophies inspired by Kant have flown under the latter ensign since John Rawls published his Dewey Lectures under the title of "Kantian Constructivism in Moral Theory" in 1980.[75] What Rawls meant by Kantian constructivism is that a conception of justice is not based on "moral truth interpreted as fixed by a prior and independent order of objects and relations, whether natural or divine, an order apart and distinct from how we conceive of ourselves," but rather is justified by "its congruence with our deeper understanding of ourselves and our aspirations, and our realization that, given our history and the traditions embedded in our public life, it is the most reasonable doctrine for us."[76] In particular, the "Kantian form of constructivism" as Rawls understands it seeks "to establish a suitable connection between a particular conception of the person and first principles of justice, by means of a procedure of construction."[77] In other words, "Kantian constructivism" is the name that Rawls used in 1980 to characterize the methodology of his *A Theory of Justice* from 1971: People committed to expressing "their nature as free and equal beings," further characterized by the two "moral powers" or abilities to form a "conception of the good" and to exercise a "sense of justice," would agree to abide by the principles of social cooperation that would be selected by impartial parties, in an "original position" behind a "veil of ignorance" about their own particular advantages or disadvantages; the thought-experiment of defining the original position and then determining what principles of justice would be selected by persons in that position is the "procedure of construction" to which Rawls subsequently refers.[78] But as even this brief account makes clear, Rawls's constructivism was a method for *political* philosophy, deriving principles of social justice from a moral conception of human beings, but not arguing for the latter itself.[79] In other words, Rawls's constructivism was not a constructivism "all the way down," in which the most fundamental principles of morality itself would be constructed from a conception of the person that is not itself nonmoral or is in some sense prior to morality. For examples of Kantian constructivism "all the way down," we have to turn to such Kantian moral philosophers as Onora

[74] The literature on constructivism is extensive and will hardly all be cited here. Several useful collections are Bagnoli 2013 and dos Santos and Schmidt 2018.

[75] Rawls 1980. [76] Rawls 1980 (1999b), pp. 306–7. [77] Rawls 1980 (1999b), p. 304.

[78] Quotations from Rawls 1999a, pp. 222, 17. For my interpretation of Rawls's approach, see Guyer 2018b, especially pp. 584–92.

[79] See also Guyer 2013.

O'Neill and Christine Korsgaard.[80] These approaches, as we saw at the outset, attempt to derive at least the most fundamental normative principle of morality in general, not just of social justice, from a conception of what it is to reason or to have a reason.

Before we can consider how the interpretation of Kant's method in moral philosophy that has been offered here maps on to the contemporary debate between constructivism and moral realism, however, we must note an ambiguity in the contrast between constructivism and its opponent, moral realism – for the "realism" in "moral realism" might mean two different things. Rawls's original contrast to constructivism in *A Theory of Justice* suggests what we might for want of a better term call an *ontological* contrast: moral realism would be a view that moral principles are based on some sort of fact or reality that exists independently of human thought or attitudes more generally, while constructivism would be the view that moral principles are generated by some internal feature of human thought or agency. But realism is also often contrasted to antirealism, in what we can for want of a better term call a *semantic* contrast: Here moral realism would be the view that moral statements have a determinate truth-value, while moral antirealism would be the view that they do not.[81]

Kant's moral philosophy is not usually described a form of *semantic* antirealism. It is clear that Kant thinks that fundamental propositions of morality such as "It is morally requisite to act only on maxims that could also be willed as universal laws" and "It is wrong to subordinate morality to self-love" are true, not false or indeterminate in truth-value. It is also clear that Kant thinks that more particular propositions such as "It is just to claim as much freedom of action for oneself as is compatible with extending an equal degree of freedom to others," "It is just to use coercion as a hindrance to a hindrance to freedom" as limited by the previous proposition (see MM-DR, Introduction, §§B and C, 6: 230–1), "It is virtuous to seek the assistance of others in the pursuit of one's own happiness only if one is willing to extend assistance to others in the pursuit of

[80] See the papers by Onora O'Neill collected in her 1989 as well as 2015, Korsgaard 1996 and 2009, and Formosa 2017, ch. 2.

[81] My distinction between semantic and ontological realism/antirealism is similar to Frederick Rauscher's distinction between empirical and transcendental moral realism and idealism. Empirical moral realism is the position that moral principles, properties, or objects of the world are independent of particular empirical moral agents, empirical moral idealism the position that they are not, while transcendental idealism would be the position that these moral facts depend on the constitution of the transcendental subject, common to all empirical persons, and transcendental moral realism the position that they have some external foundation. Rauscher defends a combination of empirical moral realism with transcendental moral idealism; see Rauscher 2015, ch. 1. I am defending semantic moral realism, ontological moral realism at the level of the fundamental principle of morality, and constructivism about particular duties.

theirs as circumstances require and permit" (MM-DV, §27, 6: 450–1), and so on, are true, not false or of indeterminate truth-value, and moreover demonstrable, derivable from the fundamental principles of morality combined with certain contingent but indisputable facts about the human condition (see MM, Introduction, section I, 6: 217). Propositions about imperfect duties with "wide latitude," such as the duties of self-perfection or to promote the happiness of others, might seem to be an exception to this claim, since in these cases it is left open precisely how one is to promote one's own self-perfection or precisely which others one should help and how much one should help them; thus it might seem that a proposition like "One should promote one's own perfection by studying today for the MCATs" would be of indeterminate truth-value. But Kant clearly believes that the general proposition that everyone must seek to perfect their natural potentials of mind and body and their moral capacities is true, neither false nor indeterminate, and further since Kant asserts that there can be conflicts among "grounds of obligation" but no actual conflicts of duties, in other words that in any situation where the concept of duty applies at all there is in fact exactly one morally correct thing to do (see MM, Introduction, section III, 6: 224), he must believe that even propositions about particular instances of imperfect duties have determinate truth values, although determining what that is requires a great deal of information and judgment, and cannot be done by any simple algorithm.

So from a semantic point of view, Kant's moral philosophy is committed to realism, not antirealism, although precisely because empirical information about human nature and the actual circumstances of human life and even particular human lives have to be employed in order to determine what our particular duties are, conclusions about such duties have to be reached by a method that could plausibly be called a procedure of construction – the truths about our particular duties are certainly not simply and immediately given by some form of intuition. That leaves the question about whether Kant's moral philosophy is really opposed to some form of realism in what I have called an ontological regard. Philosophers such as Korsgaard, who holds that the fundamental principle of morality can be derived from the commitments of agency, or O'Neill, who holds it can be derived from a purely procedural conception of reasoning, think that Kantian moral philosophy is opposed to some form of ontological realism about moral values.[82] But interpreters such as Allen Wood, Karl Ameriks, and my own past self, who hold that Kant's moral philosophy is founded upon the claim that humanity *is* an end in itself, or that

[82] Rauscher describes O'Neill as a procedural constructivist, and notes that Korsgaard sometimes calls her position proceduralist, even "procedural realism," but more often "describes her position as one of a constitution of agency"; Rauscher 2015, pp. 24n25, 26n30.

human freedom is *intrinsically* valuable, are committed to a form of moral realism: the *value* of humanity or of freedom is supposed be a fact that obtains independently of our belief in it, although we ought to believe it.[83] I have previously taken a realist attitude toward the *value* of humanity;[84] here, however, I have been arguing that Kant's derivation of the fundamental principle of morality proceeds by the application of the principle of noncontradiction to the *fact* that every human being has a will of his or her own, in the form of the idea that to act immorally is both to assert and deny that the object of such action, whether oneself or another, has its own will. This is a fact, in Kant's own terminology a "fact of reason," but it is not a mysterious *moral* fact, or a *value* that somehow exists in the universe independently of our act of valuing it. It is simply a fact that cannot be denied on pain of self-contradiction, since, Kant assumes, in some way we always recognize it even when by our actions we would deny it. Whether Kant has succeeded in *demonstrating* this fact is a question; but there is no question that he regards our possession of wills as a fact from which moral theory must begin. Thus we can say that as regards its fundamental principle, Kant's moral philosophy is a form of realism, though not specifically moral realism.[85] The specific duties of human beings may then be regarded as being constructed, or in Kant's own term reached by "inference" (*Folgerung*) from this principle by the addition of empirical facts about human nature and circumstances (again, MM, Introduction, section I, 6: 217). Thus, as Larry Krasnoff has written, "Kant's practical philosophy has what seem to be both realist and constructivist elements,"[86] although we do not need a special concept of *moral* realism, as Krasnoff too supposes, in order to understand the fact on which Kant's further construction of human duties is based.

The application of the word "realism" to any aspect of Kant's philosophy may raise hackles. More precisely, although Kant himself describes his epistemological position as "empirical realism" combined with "transcendental idealism" (CPR A371), the present account of his moral philosophy seems to present it as founded precisely upon a *transcendentally realist* claim about human beings, the claim that they do not merely *appear* each to have a will of their own, but

[83] For this contrast between the approaches of O'Neill and Korsgaard on the one hand and of Wood, Ameriks, and myself on the other, as well as references to representative works, see Krasnoff 2013, at pp. 87–9.

[84] See Guyer 1998.

[85] Thus I am distinguishing my position here not only from some of my own earlier work but also from the position of Julian Wuerth, who interprets Kant's position as a strong form of ontological moral realism, in which the moral law is immediately given along with our knowledge of our own active, noumenal selves. See Wuerth 2014, pp. 318–31. My approach here has been that for Kant only our possession of wills and the principle of noncontradiction have to be regarded as given.

[86] Krasnoff 2013, p. 89.

that they *really do*. But whether or not his own epistemological scruples should have prevented Kant from asserting this, it is precisely what he does assert in both the *Groundwork* and the *Critique of Practical Reason*. In the *Groundwork*, as we saw, Kant maintains that "a human being really finds in himself a capacity by which he distinguishes himself from all other things, even from himself insofar as he is affected by objects" (that is, himself as appearance), "and that is **reason**," which is understood in turn as "pure self-activity" – or will (G 6: 452). In the *Critique of Practical Reason*, Kant asserts that "We can become aware of pure practical laws just as we are aware of pure theoretical principles, by attending to the necessity with which reason prescribes them to us," and that "The concept of a pure will arises from the first" so that "morality first discloses to us the concept of freedom" (CPrR 5: 30), more precisely not just the concept of our freedom but the *fact* of our freedom – or our will. Kant's moral philosophy, although constructivist as contrasted, say, to intuitionist, in its *derivation* of duties, is founded upon realism, indeed transcendental realism, about the existence of will or freedom in every human being, and about the law of noncontradiction that generates the moral law from this fact.

We may now not be much tempted by Kant's transcendental realism, but then again we may not be much tempted by his transcendental idealism.[87] If we are tempted by the general approach of Kant's moral philosophy, we might want to ground it upon some more modest, empirical claim that human beings each have their own will. But if we want to preserve the structure of Kant's theory at all, we will have to accept the reality of the human will on the basis of some theory or other. Then we can go on to the derivation or construction of more specific human duties.

8 Conclusion

In the previous section, I argued that Kant's own application of his strategy for a derivation of the fundamental principle and complete object of morality from his conception of rationality ultimately presupposes insight into the noumenal reality of the human capacity to set ends, but suggested that from a contemporary point of view we might be more inclined to apply Kant's conception of rationality to the empirically known fact that human beings have such a capacity. If we do that, then we may also be inclined to think that it is a contingent matter whether any particular member of *Homo sapiens* actually has this capacity, and that the degree to which any individual human

[87] For my own most recent critique of transcendental idealism, see Guyer 2017. The foremost defender of transcendental idealism, although of what I regarded as a watered-down form of what Kant himself intended, has been Henry Allison; see Allison 2004.

being has this capacity can vary among persons and over the lifetime of any individual person – obviously people do not actualize this capacity at birth, some gradually realize it better than others, and some unfortunately lose it, gradually or suddenly, due to injury, illness, or age. These indisputable empirical facts might make the application of Kant's fundamental principle of morality, which presupposes that every human being has his or her own will just as much as every other, more complicated than Kant envisioned. Perhaps morality should be based on recognition of the fact that humans generally have free wills in the prime of life, not that every human being has a free will at every moment of life. But working out the details of applying Kant's theory under this assumption would go well beyond interpreting Kant, so I will content myself with this hint here.

But the question of whether the application of Kant's general conception of morality might involve matters of degree appears in another context as well. Here I have in mind Kant's inference from the highest good as the rational object of morality to the postulates of pure reason that are supposed to guarantee its possibility, and thus the rationality of our acting to realize it. The question here is just how Kant's principle that "ought implies can" should be applied: Should it allow us to infer that the realization of this unconditioned good must really be possible, although it does not seem to be so in mere nature and instead requires our acceptance of the reality of immortality and God? Or should the demand of reason be taken to be, as Kant suggests in a perhaps unguarded statement in the essay "On the Common Saying: That May Be Correct in Theory But Is of No Use in Practice" (1793), that what morality and thus reason itself requires of us is only "to work *to the best of one's ability* toward the **highest good** *possible in the world*" (TP 8: 279, italics added)? Although Kant goes on here to make his usual claim that making our pursuit of this goal rational "exacts from reason belief, **for practical purposes**, in a moral ruler of the world and in a future life," one might well argue that the requirement to work *to the best of our ability* to the highest good *possible in the world* does not require any superhuman efforts possible only in another world than that of our actual experience, rather *only that we really do make the best efforts possible for actual human beings in nature as it actually is*. That would be to infer from a limit on what we can do to a restriction on what we can be obliged to do, rather than inferring an unrestricted capacity to do what morality would entail *under ideal circumstances* to a capacity to perform beyond all reasonable but empirical expectations. Even doing the best that we actually can under the empirically given, actual circumstances of human life may require a lot more from us than we often, lazily and self-servingly, think we can do. I for one would be content to think that this is all that reason requires of us, for it is plenty.

Bibliography

A Note on Translation and Citations to the Works of Kant

Translations from Kant's works are from the Cambridge Edition volumes listed in the Bibliography. On the model of Kant's own typography, Kant's emphasis is indicated by **boldface**. The following abbreviations are used: Anth = *Anthropology from a Pragmatic Point of View*; CJ = *Critique of the Power of Judgment*; CPrR = *Critique of Practical Reason*; CPR = *Critique of Pure Reason*; G = *Groundwork for the Metaphysics of Morals*; JL = *Jäsche Logic*; MM = Metaphysics of Morals (DV = Doctrine of Virtue/DR = Doctrine of Right); Eth-C = *Moral Philosophy Collins*; L-NR = *Naturrecht Feyerabend*; Refl = *Reflexion;* Rel = *Religion within the Boundaries of Mere Reason*; TP = "On the Common Saying: That May Be Correct in Theory But It Is of No Use in Practice." The volume and page numbers of the *Akademie* edition are used, except for the *Critique of Pure Reason*, for which the pagination of its first ("A") and second ("B") editions are used. Kant used roman type for Latin words; I use italics for those as well as for my own emphasis.

I Kant's Works

Kant, Immanuel (1900–). *Kants gesammelte Schriften*. Edited by the Royal Prussian (later German, then Berlin-Brandenburg) Academy of Sciences. 29 vols. Berlin: Georg Reimer (later Walter de Gruyter). (*Akademie* edition)

Kant, Immanuel (1992). *Lectures on Logic*. Edited and translated by J. Michael Young. Cambridge: Cambridge University Press.

Kant, Immanuel (1993). *Theoretical Philosophy, 1755–1770*. Edited and translated by David E. Walford in collaboration with Ralf Meerbote. Cambridge: Cambridge University Press.

Kant, Immanuel (1996a). *Practical Philosophy*. Edited and translated by Mary J. Gregor. Cambridge: Cambridge University Press.

Kant, Immanuel (1996b). *Religion and Rational Theology*. Edited and translated by Allen W. Wood and George di Giovanni. Cambridge: Cambridge University Press.

Kant, Immanuel (1997). *Lectures on Ethics*. Edited by Peter Heath and J. B. Schneewind, translated by Peter Heath. Cambridge: Cambridge University Press.

Kant, Immanuel (1998). *Critique of Pure Reason*. Edited and translated by Paul Guyer and Allen W. Wood. Cambridge: Cambridge University Press.

Kant, Immanuel (2000). *Critique of the Power of Judgment*. Edited by Paul Guyer, translated by Paul Guyer and Eric Matthews. Cambridge: Cambridge University Press.

Kant, Immanuel (2004). *Vorlesung zur Moralphilosophie*. Edited by Werner Stark and Manfred Kuehn. Berlin and New York: Walter de Gruyter.

Kant, Immanuel (2005). *Notes and Fragments*. Edited by Paul Guyer, translated by Curtis Bowman, Paul Guyer, and Frederick Rauscher. Cambridge: Cambridge University Press.

Kant, Immanuel (2006). *Anthropology, History, and Education*. Edited by Robert B. Louden and Günter Zöller. Cambridge: Cambridge University Press.

Kant, Immanuel (2016). *Lectures and Drafts on Political Philosophy*. Edited by Frederick Rauscher, translated by Frederick Rauscher and Kenneth R. Westphal. Cambridge: Cambridge University Press.

II Other Primary Sources

Hume, David (1739–40). *A Treatise of Human Nature*. Ed. David Fate and Mary J. Norton. 2 vols. Oxford: Clarendon Press, 2009.

Leibniz, Gottfried Wilhelm (1969). *Philosophical Papers and Letters*. Translated and edited by Leroy E. Loemker. Dordrecht: D. Reidel.

Meier, Georg Friedrich (1762–74). *Philosophische Sittenlehre*. Second, improved edition. 5 vols. Halle: Carl Hermann Hemmerde.

Meier, Georg Friedrich (1764). *Allgemeine practische Weltweisheit*. Magdeburg: Carl Hermann Hemmerde.

Meier, Georg Friedrich (2016). *Excerpt from the Doctrine of Reason*. Trans. Aaron Bunch, in collaboration with Axel Gelfert and Ricardo Pozzo. London: Bloomsbury.

Ross, David (1930). *The Right and the Good*. Oxford: Clarendon Press.

Schopenhauer, Arthur (2009). *Prize Essay on the Basis of Morals*, in *The Two Fundamental Problems of Ethics*. Translated and edited by Christopher Janaway. Cambridge: Cambridge University Press.

Schopenhauer, Arthur. (2010). *The World as Will and Representation*. 2nd ed. Edited by Judith Norman, Alistair Welchman, and Christopher Janaway. Cambridge: Cambridge University Press.

Sidgwick, Henry (1888). "The Kantian Conception of Free Will," *Mind* XIII (1888): 405–12. Reprinted in *The Methods of Ethics*, 7th ed. (London: Macmillan, 1907), pp. 511–16.

Ulrich, Johann August Heinrich (1788). *Eleutheriologie oder über Freiheit und Nothwendigkeit*. Jena: Cröker.

III Secondary Sources

Allison, Henry E. (1990). *Kant's Theory of Freedom*. Cambridge: Cambridge University Press.

Allison, Henry E. (2004). *Kant's Transcendental Idealism: An Interpretation and Defense*. 2nd ed. New Haven and London: Yale University Press.

Allison, Henry E. (2011). *Kant's* Groundwork for the Metaphysics of Morals: *A Commentary*. Oxford: Oxford University Press.

Bagnoli, Carla, ed. (2013). *Constructivism in Ethics*. Cambridge: Cambridge University Press.

Busch, Werner (1979). *Entstehung der kritischen Rechtsphilosophie Kants. Kant-Studien Ergänzungshefte* 110. Berlin and New York: Walter de Gruyter.

Cummiskey, David (1996). *Kantian Consequentialism*. New York: Oxford University Press.

dos Santos, Robinson, and Elke Elisabeth Schmidt, eds. (2018). *Realism and Antirealism in Kant's Moral Philosophy. Kant-Studien Erganzungshefte* 199. Berlin and Boston: Walter de Gruyter.

Formosa, Paul (2017). *Kantian Ethics, Dignity and Perfection*. Cambridge: Cambridge University Press, 2017.

Forster, Michael N. (2008). *Kant and Skepticism*. Princeton: Princeton University Press.

Guyer, Paul (1987). *Kant and the Claims of Knowledge*. Cambridge: Cambridge University Press.

Guyer, Paul (1992). *The Cambridge Companion to Kant*. Cambridge: Cambridge University Press.

Guyer, Paul (1995). "The Possibility of the Categorical Imperative," *Philosophical Review* 104: 353–85. Reprinted in Guyer, *Kant on Freedom, Law, and Happiness* (Cambridge: Cambridge University Press, 2000), pp. 172–206.

Guyer, Paul (1997). "From a Practical Point of View: Kant's Conception of a Postulate of Pure Practical Reason." *Philosophisches Jahrbuch* 104: 1–18. Reprinted in Guyer 2000, pp. 333–71.

Guyer, Paul (1998). "The Value of Reason and the Value of Freedom." *Ethics* 109: 22–35.

Guyer, Paul (2000). *Kant on Freedom, Law, and Happiness*. Cambridge: Cambridge University Press.

Guyer, Paul (2001). "From Nature to Morality: Kant's New Argument in the 'Critique of Teleological Judgment'." Pp. 375–404 in Hans-Friedrich Fulda and Jürgen Stoltzenberg, eds., *Architektonik und System in der*

Philosophie Kants. Hamburg: Felix Meiner Verlag. Reprinted in Guyer 2005, pp. 314–42.

Guyer, Paul (2002). "Kant's Deductions of the Principles of Right." Pp. 24–64 in Mark Timmons, ed., *Kant's* Metaphysics of Morals*: Interpretative Essays*. Oxford: Oxford University Press. Reprinted in Guyer 2005, pp. 198–242.

Guyer, Paul (2003). "Kant on Common Sense and Skepticism," *Kantian Review* 7 (2003): 1–37. Reprinted in Guyer 2008a, pp. 23–70.

Guyer, Paul (2005). *Kant's System of Nature and Freedom: Selected Essays*. Oxford: Clarendon Press.

Guyer, Paul (2006). *The Cambridge Companion to Kant and Modern Philosophy*. Cambridge: Cambridge University Press.

Guyer, Paul (2007a). *Kant's* Groundwork for the Metaphysics of Morals: *A Reader's Guide*. London: Continuum.

Guyer, Paul (2007b). "Naturalistic and Transcendental Moments in Kant's Moral Philosophy." *Inquiry* 50 (2007): 444–64.

Guyer, Paul (2008a). *Knowledge, Reason, and Taste: Kant's Response to Hume*. Princeton: Princeton University Press.

Guyer, Paul (2008b). "Proving Ourselves Free." Pp. 115–37 in Valerio Rhoden, Ricardo R. Terra, Guido de Almeida, and Margit Ruffings, eds. *Recht und Frieden in der Philosophie Kants: Akten des X. Internationalen Kant-Kongresses*. 5 vols. Berlin and New York: Walter de Gruyter. Vol. 1. Reprinted in Guyer 2016a, pp. 146–62.

Guyer, Paul (2009a). "Problems with Freedom: Kant's Argument in *Groundwork* III and its Subsequent Emendation." Pp. 176–202 in Jens Timmermann, ed., *Kant's* Groundwork of the Metaphysics of Morals*: A Critical Guide*. Cambridge: Cambridge University Press.

Guyer, Paul (2009b). "Is and Ought: From Hume to Kant, and Now." In German in Heiner F. Klemme, ed., *Kant und die Zukunft der Aufklarung*. Berlin and New York: Walter de Gruyter, pp. 210–32. Translated in Guyer 2016a, pp. 21–25.

Guyer, Paul (2011). "Kantian Communities." Pp. 88–120 in Charlton Payne and Lucas Thorpe, eds., *Kant and the Concept of Community*, North American Kant Society Studies in Philosophy 9. Rochester: University of Rochester Press. Reprinted in Guyer 2016a, pp. 275–302.

Guyer, Paul (2013). "Constructivism and Self-Constitution." Pp. 176–200 in Mark Timmons and Sorin Baiasu, eds., *Kant on Practical Justification: Interpretive Essays*. Oxford: Oxford University Press.

Guyer, Paul (2014). *Kant*, 2nd ed. (London: Routledge, 2014), chapter 5, pp. 203–41.

Guyer, Paul (2016a). *Virtues of Freedom: Selected Essays on Kant*. Oxford: Oxford University Press.

Guyer, Paul (2016b). "Kant, Mendelssohn, and Immortality." Pp. 157–79 in Thomas Höwing, ed., *The Highest Good in Kant's Philosophy*. Berlin and Boston: Walter de Gruyter.

Guyer, Paul (2016c). "The Twofold Morality of *Recht*: Once More Unto the Breach." *Kant-Studien* 107: 34–63.

Guyer, Paul (2017). "Transcendental Idealism: What and Why?" Pp. 71–90 in Matthew C. Altman, ed., *The Palgrave Kant Handbook*. London: Palgrave Macmillan.

Guyer, Paul (2018a). "The Struggle for Freedom: Freedom of Will in Kant and Reinhold." Pp. 120–37 in Eric Watkins, ed., *Kant on Persons and Agency*. Cambridge: Cambridge University Press.

Guyer, Paul (2018b). "Principles of Justice, Primary Goods, and Categories of Right: Rawls and Kant." *Kantian Review* 23: 581–613.

Herman, Barbara (1993). *The Practice of Moral Judgment*. Cambridge, MA: Harvard University Press.

Korsgaard, Christine M. (1986). "Kant's Formula of Universal Law," *Kant-Studien* 77 (1986): 183–202. Reprinted in Korsgaard 1996a, pp. 77–105.

Korsgaard, Christine M. (1989). "Kant's Analysis of Obligation: The Argument of *Groundwork* I." *Monist* 72 (1989): 311–40. Reprinted in Korsgaard 1996a, pp. 43–76.

Korsgaard, Christine M. (1996a). *Creating the Kingdom of Ends*. Cambridge: Cambridge University Press.

Korsgaard, Christine M. (1996b). *The Sources of Normativity*. Edited by Onora O'Neill. Cambridge: Cambridge University Press.

Korsgaard, Christine M. (2009). *Self-Constitution: Agency, Identity, and Integrity*. Oxford: Oxford University Press.

Krasnoff, Larry (2013). "Constructing Practical Justification: How Can the Categorical Imperative Justify Desire-based Actions?" Pp. 87–109 in Mark Timmons and Sorin Baiasu, eds., *Kant on Practical Justification*. Oxford: Oxford Univesity Press.

Nagel, Thomas (1970). *The Possibility of Altruism*. Oxford: Clarendon Press.

O'Neill, Onora (1989). *Constructions of Reason: Explorations of Kant's Practical Philosophy*. Cambridge: Cambridge University Press.

O'Neill, Onora (1992). "Vindicating Reason." Originally in Guyer 1992, pp. 280–308. Reprinted in O'Neill 2015, pp. 13–37.

O'Neill, Onora (2004). "Autonomy, Plurality and Public Reason." Pp. 181–94 in Natalie Brender and Larry Krasnoff, eds., *New Essays on the History of*

Autonomy: A Collection Honoring J.B. Schneewind. Cambridge: Cambridge University Press.

O'Neill, Onora (2013). *Acting on Principle: An Essay on Kantian Ethics*. 2nd ed. Cambridge: Cambridge University Press.

O'Neill, Onora (2015). *Constructing Authorities: Reason, Politics and Interpretation in Kant's Philosophy*. Cambridge: Cambridge University Press.

Piper, Adrian M. S. (1997). "Kant on the Objectivity of the Moral Law." Pp. 240–69 in Andrews Reath, Barbara Herman, and Christine M. Korsgaard, eds. *Reclaiming the History of Ethics: Essays for John Rawls*. Cambridge: Cambridge University Press.

Piper, Adrian M. S. (2012). "Kant's Self-Legislation Procedure Reconsidered." *Kant Studies Online*, pp. 203–77.

Piper, Adrian M. S. (2013). *Rationality and the Structure of the Self*, 2nd ed. 2 vols. Berlin: APRA Foundation.

Piper, Adrian M. S. (2018). "The Logic of Kant's Categorical 'Imperative'." Pp. 2037–46 in Violetta L. Waibel, Margit Ruffing, and David Wagner, eds., *Natur und Freiheit: Akten des XII. Internationalen Kant-Kongresses*. 5 vols. Berlin and Boston: Walter de Gruyter. Vol. 3.

Rauscher, Frederick (2015). *Naturalism and Realism in Kant's Ethics*. Cambridge: Cambridge University Press.

Rawls, John (1980). "Kantian Constructivism in Moral Theory." *Journal of Philosophy* 77: 515–72. Reprinted in Rawls 1999b, *Collected Papers*, ed. Samuel Freeman. Cambridge, MA: Harvard University Press, pp. 303–58.

Rawls, John (1999a). *A Theory of Justice*, revised edition. Cambridge, MA: Harvard University Press.

Rawls, John (1999b). *Collected Papers*, ed. Samuel Freeman. Cambridge, MA: Harvard University Press.

Rawls, John (2000). *Lectures on the History of Moral Philosophy*. Edited by Barbara Herman. Cambridge, MA: Harvard University Press.

Schneewind, J. B. (2010). "Voluntarism and the Foundations of Ethics." Pp. 202–21 in Schneewind, *Essays on the History of Moral Philosophy*. Oxford: Oxford University Press.

Wood, Allen W. (1999). *Kant's Ethical Thought*. Cambridge: Cambridge University Press.

Wood, Allen W. (2001). "The Moral Law as a System of Formulas." Pp. 287–306 in Hans-Friedrich Fulda and Jürgen Stolzenberg, eds., *Architektonik und System in der Philosophie Kants*. Hamburg: Felix Meiner Verlag.

Wood, Allen W. (2006). "The Supreme Principle of Morality." In Guyer 2006, pp. 342–80.

Wood, Allen W. (2008). *Kantian Ethics*. Cambridge: Cambridge University Press.

Wood, Allen W. (2014). *The Free Development of Each: Studies on Freedom, Right, and Ethics in Classical German Philosophy*. Oxford: Oxford University Press.

Wood, Allen W. (2017). *Formulas of the Moral Law*. Cambridge: Cambridge University Press.

Wuerth, Julian (2014). *Kant on Mind, Action, and Ethics*. Oxford: Oxford University Press.

Acknowledgments

This Element is based on a paper originally presented at the Tel Aviv Ben Gurion University Conference "Critical Connections" organized by Yakir Levine and Yaron Senderowicz; Patricia Kitcher asked me a particularly helpful question on that occasion. I subsequently presented the material at a seminar at the University of Basel hosted by Gunnar Hindrichs, who had valuable suggestions. I presented the core argument of the current Element to a joint colloquium of the Departments of Philosophy and Logic and Philosophy of Science at the University of California, Irvine; there Jeremy Heis asked me a useful question. The editors of the Cambridge Elements series, Desmond Hogan, Allen Wood, and Howard Williams, all gave me useful comments. I am particularly grateful to Adrian Piper, who read the entire manuscript with care and gave me many valuable comments and criticisms.

Cambridge Elements

The Philosophy of Immanuel Kant

About the Series

This Cambridge Elements series provides an extensive overview of Kant's philosophy and its impact upon philosophy and philosophers. Distinguished Kant specialists will provide an up-to-date summary of the results of current research in their fields and give their own take on what they believe are the most significant debates influencing research, drawing original conclusions.

Cambridge Elements

The Philosophy of Immanuel Kant

Elements in the Series

A full series listing is available at: www.cambridge.org/EPIK

Printed in the United States
By Bookmasters